BUSINESS

THAT CARE

COMPILED AND EDITED BY

CANDACE GISH &
APRILLE JANES

ZANDER

Livonia, Michigan

Published by Zander
an imprint of BHC Press

Library of Congress Control Number:
2017945131

ISBN-13: 978-1-946848-49-9
ISBN-10: 1-946848-49-2

Visit the publisher at:
www.bhcpress.com

Also available in ebook

TABLE OF CONTENTS

This book is dedicated to my four
amazing Diva Daughters
who inspire me each and every day
to be the best version of me.

Also to all the extraordinary women
in this world that are about to tap
into their greatness so they can
live their lives to the fullest.

FOREWORD
by Jo Dibblee

When Candace asked me to write the forward for this book I was an unabashed YES!

I am a firm believer in being the change and being a part of others lives and stories! I am honored to write the forward. The stories resonate and remind me of the journey of life—the human experience.

The worst possible thing a person can do is settle for a life of less than. Or buy into the belief they are not worthy of something bigger and better—something uniquely destined for them.

First and foremost, we have all been there: felt less than, broken and bruised. It's part of the human experience. Plain and simple, that's life.

It does not matter from which you come—not at all. What is important in life is where you end. Buying into anything less than that limits you and subdues your light in the world. And that, my friend, is a tragedy that no one should ever accept as truth.

I know this to be true. Having been a witness in a murder investigation I spent 35 years in hiding. Many times, I was broken, bruised and a puddle on the floor of life. Trust me when I tell you it wasn't pretty.

One day enough was enough, and I was sick and tired of being sick and tired, of living a lie, a less-than life and worse, a life of simply existing. For me, that was 2007.

You see, Dear Reader, one day you will come to the end of the line or reach your point of demarcation when you decide to change what needs changing and claim back YOU!

And that is what this book is all about. It's the stories of women who have stood and decided to live the life they dreamt of, to make their mark in whatever way is meaningful to them!

In these pages, you will find stories of inspiration and reclamations but you will also see yourself and your journey, and that is what a good collection should deliver.

Candace Gish, a woman of integrity and purpose, is heart-centered and passion-driven to be the change she wants to see in this world and it is evident in all she does!

To all the women who have shared openly and freely, I salute you for your courage, truth, and openness.

One person can be the change, and these women have decided to share in being the change!

Life, by definition, is a verb. It's not static but dynamic, whether we like it or not. Since change is the one real constant, why not live the life you dream about?

So, dive in and fill your cup. The stories are short and sweet and offer gems of learning and inspiration! And when you have filled your cup to the brim—get up and get moving toward your very own delicious life!

Jo Dibblee is the Founder of Frock Off Inc., and author of internationally-awarded *Frock Off— Living Undisguised*

Divas ARE...

DETERMINED
TO REACH THEIR GOALS

INDIVIDUALS
WHO CELEBRATE THEIR UNIQUENESS

VICTORIOUS
IN CONQUERING THEIR FEARS

ALWAYS
RESPECTFUL OF OTHERS

SOMEONE
TO RELY ON

AN INTRODUCTION
by Divas That Care

The idea for this series of anthologies was birthed on a vacation that revealed the vast difference between the haves and the have-nots on our planet. Candace Gish came home from that trip hungry to use her business and radio show to make a difference. When she looked around for inspiration and support on how to do that, she couldn't find anything. So, like any good entrepreneur worth her sale, she decided to create it herself.

The vision of this anthology is to bring together a community of committed women. Women who have ideas and strategies on how we can work together to make our world a better place, not just for ourselves but also for future generations.

A movement of Divas That Care!

When I was young and free and my imagination had no limits

I dreamt of changing the world.

As I grew older and wiser, I discovered the world would not change.

I shortened my sights and decided to change my country,

But it too seemed immovable.

As I grew into my twilight years, in one last desperate attempt

I settled for changing my family,

But alas, they would have none of it.

And now as I lay on my deathbed, I realize:

If I had changed myself first

Then, by example I would have changed my family.

From their inspiration and encouragement,

I would have been able to change my country

And who knows, I may even have changed the world.

Adapted from an epitaph in Westminster, Anonymous

TO OUR MOVEMENT
CHANGE BEGINS WITH US

We do not need magic to change the world,
we carry all the power we need inside ourselves
already: we have the power to imagine better.

~ J.K. Rowling ~

LIFE'S INSPIRATIONS
by Candace Gish

When I first started thinking about putting a book together featuring Divas from my radio show, I felt excited and scared. I never thought of myself as a writer and wondered if I could pull it off. For years I saw myself as the "middle person" in a lot of ways, a facilitator.

This journey started six years ago because of someone who believed in me and pushed me out of my comfort zone. I remember clearly the day one of my mentors approached me, asking me to interview some women she knew in business, on her internet radio show.

It was one of the most terrifying requests I've ever received. Even more frightening than when I went skydiving.

Before sharing with you my mission for this *Diva That Cares* anthology, I want to convey my vision for the Divas That Care movement. It has grown from my passion to create a platform for women to use their voices and share a message. I believe in their greatness and that one passionate person can change the world for the better. I believe in possibilities and whether you are 8 or 88, if you have something to share, I want to help you.

My vision is big!

We plan to sell The *Divas That Care* book series on a global scale. Some of the contributing authors will inspire large audiences and create huge impact. Others will work in their local communities while still others will motivate friends and family to act. Each one of us, working in our chosen sphere of influence, can transform the world, one person at a time.

As the founder of this inspired movement, I will continue to bring together passionate women and spread the message.

While attending a swim practise for my four daughters, ages 14, 12, 11 and 8, I sat in the stands and reflected on all we have done together over the years. I started homeschooling my daughters nine years ago when my oldest, Lexi, was in grade 1 and our youngest wasn't even born.

Homeschooling is fantastic, don't get me wrong but it was not something I ever saw myself doing with my family. At the time I began, it was a necessity because we felt let down by the school system. It was intended to be a short-term solution that ended up long-term. I don't regret a moment of it and along the way have learned so much about myself.

The respect I have for teachers is so much stronger now as I teach my girls. What I have learned from this experience is how important it is to really get to know who people are at their core so we can accept and honor the differences in each of us.

We all see the world differently; our journeys are unique and no two are the same. The Divas on the program are true examples of this and I love how they share their wisdom with the listeners. I am also grateful that the interviews are recorded. As my girls get older they will benefit from listening to these fantastic women.

As I watch my four beautiful daughters go through the homeschool process, I encourage them to be themselves, to follow their dreams and always to help others. Accepting each other for who we truly are is something to aspire to. I am my daughters' biggest cheerleader and I love being a cheerleader to all our Divas.

My girls and I have shared many road trips across North American for up to six weeks at a time. They have probably seen more of Canada and the United States then most people. These experiences—from visiting California to the Great Lakes and monuments like Mt Rushmore and historic battlefields—have encouraged and fostered our curiosity. Curiosity is how we all learn.

When I was a child, I loved to sit and just watch people. I wasn't shy, just quiet in my own way. I always wanted to be that proverbial fly on a wall, buzzing around to see what people were doing. My dad John, took me everywhere, from his friends' homes to his sports events.

I loved how he interacted with people and he became my hero in so many ways. Always respectful, kind and caring to people, Dad gave them his full attention and made them feel important. Family was always most important thing to him and he made me feel like a princess.

My dad's family was mostly in Ontario, Canada while we lived in Alberta, Canada, so he also taught me that family is not just blood. He showed me you can make a family from great friends. My dad has amazing friends I consider to be my family even today, especially my godmother Nancy.

In many ways, it is my dad's influence that started my journey of service to others. In school, I always wanted to assist where I could. That led me to volunteering later at the youth center, then victim services, local community boards, the Royal Purple, The Legion and many other charities. I felt it was my responsibility to do this and I have passed that on to my daughters.

My mother Pat is also a huge influence in my life. Bigger than life, I learned through her example what it means to be independent. Always the entrepreneur, I idolized her for the determination and motivation she modelled by always striving to be the best she could be.

I witnessed her and her family's struggles with health. Never one to give up, she showed me if you want something bad enough or if you don't like the outcome you were given, it's up to you to do something about it. Pat did this by reinventing herself. She went back to school and learned what she could to do to help improve, not just her own health, but also the health of others. (You can read her story in Chapter 10.)

Today she works with thousands of individuals and I am so proud of who she has become. The day she married my stepdad Jim was one of my happiest days. I now have a wonderful brother Dana who is truly a wonderful, unique and loving person.

My journey to inspire and motivate others started with my remarkable parents, but does not end there. Through them over the years, I met incredible mentors and kindred spirits who shared similar passions. These individuals lead me to focus a lot on my own personal development and to find out who I was.

In my twenties, I met a very remarkable man named Kevin, who would later become my husband. Kevin inspires me with his loyalty and giving spirit. He is a strong man who is always questioning and challenging me, the ying to my yang, but always in my corner. Through his strong support and belief in me, I can focus on raising our four daughters and continue to develop Divas That Care.

These astonishing Divas that I interview weekly, inspire me with their powerful stories. They are leaving an imprint on the world, and this has encouraged me to climb Mt Kilimanjaro in 2019 with my friend Brenda, to raise money for Type 1 Diabetes. The excitement of flying across the world for the first time to hike one of the highest points is also daunting.

For myself, the journey leading up to summiting the mountain will be the most meaningful. I'm doing this as my contribution to the Divas That Care movement because I want to inspire others to act on their passions as well.

I am beyond excited to share all of this with my daughters Lexi, Arwen, Josie and Harlee. This book you hold in your hands is just the start of a greater legacy in the *Divas That Care* series. My wish for you is that you enjoy the stories and messages from each of these authors as much as I have enjoyed being connecting with them and bringing them to you. All of them are inspiring in so many ways and have poured themselves into their chapters.

The Divas That Cares movement, book and mission is to *support, inspire, and engage a community of committed women by offering ideas and strategies on how we can work together to make the world a better place. Not just for ourselves but also for future generations.*

Thank you, Aprille, for making this all happen. With your help, we can move mountains.

To all our Divas, thank you for being a part of this journey with us!

ABOUT CANDACE GISH

As an independent business woman herself, Candace Gish understands the challenges women face in business and how to be successful. That's why she also understands the importance of having mentors and a strong support network.

Today, her four daughters and wonderful husband inspire her to work for a better world. She loves connecting with women who have big dreams and the commitment to make a difference.

She believes in the power of women when they come together to effect change.

That's what the Divas That Care movement is all about.

When she's not talking with the Divas on her radio show, building her network marketing business, homeschooling her four daughters or volunteering, you will find her curled up with a great book, doing traditional rug hooking, gardening or traveling.

You can listen to current and past episodes of Candace's radio show at: www.DivasThatCare.com

STEP ONE

Reject

THE OLD MESSAGING

It's not the absence of fear, it's overcoming it.
Sometimes you've got to blast through and have faith.

~ Emma Watson ~

SURVIVE OR THRIVE?
by Amy McKenzie

When I consider the notion of surviving versus thriving, it generates what has become a foundational question in my own personal development; "Who am I being?"

In my view, whether we provide a service, run a business, or author a story that moves a multitude, at the end of the day all that really matters is who we have become. When we allow our agenda to take precedence over people, or trade our humanity for personal gain, then I say, our measure for success deserves scrutiny.

Ambition ruled my choices for years. My background is in professional theatre where success hangs on the opinions of others. Personal satisfaction is immaterial, a standing ovation, a five-star review or the ultimate validation, a Tony Award, determine one's value. My drive to prove my worthiness was running the show, *my* show.

Over time my focus on personal development shed light on how vacant one's life becomes when fixated on survival. Everything I once recognized as significant diminished in value and I saw that true success in life is making a difference for the person standing in front of you. To leave people with an experience of their own greatness became my goal. Outwardly it appears simple, like leaving

25

the bank teller smiling or the customer service agent happier when you disconnect.

When I forget and my agenda becomes more important than people, I no longer have an experience of thriving. At those times, to quote a wonderful mentor, Jim Bunch, I have allowed myself to drop into, "below the line thinking," where fear fuels our emotional state. Below the line thinking rarely inspires love, compassion or forgiveness.

What keeps us from plummeting below the line? If I could discover the answer to this I might achieve the quality of life I sought.

By becoming acutely aware of my ongoing conversation with myself, and listening for what people were saying about themselves, a pattern emerged. The one commonality was the words we use. Everything we experience emanates from the words we choose. In fact, it is our very words that define us.

Upon acknowledging that words have visceral power, the influence of these two simple words, "I am," stood out to me. I began observing what follows. When you say, "I am _____," notice what's automatically present. It's likely familiar and is quite possibly running *your* show.

For example, think of someone you know that says, "I am always late." Do you notice they are generally correct? Well, that's because we get to be right about what we declare. Conversely, if you are someone who says, "I am always on time," you begin to arrange your life in a way that supports keeping your word. Over time, as you effectively execute what you set out to do, your view of yourself shifts and your confidence increases. Trusting ourselves to be a match for the person we "say" we are a pathway to accomplishing greater self-worth and a sense of inner peace. And ultimately our greatest access to designing a life we love.

In the process of focusing on my choices consciously I developed a system, culled from many disciplines, to aid me in acquiring greater awareness. I call it the Lighthouse Technique.

Step One: Close your eyes and mentally construct a lighthouse in your mind.

Step Two: Imagine climbing the stairs until you reach the viewing deck.

Step Three: Practice looking down and watching yourself as you play out the scenes of your life.

As you watch, ask yourself, "Is this the story I had in mind for myself?" If you had instant replay, would you be content? With practice, perceiving yourself from this view, it becomes easier to hit pause and consider your actions before dropping into a patterned response.

Taking this pause between the heartbeats, if you will, allows one to redirect the neural pathways and create a new, conscious response. Or as another dear mentor, Geoffrey Bullington, terms it, "avoid dropping into the Grand Canyon of the mind."

During my career, I was asked to take on teaching inner-city teenagers who'd been placed in a Juvenile Detention home. Having worked closely with the late, great Paul Sills of Second City and Saturday Night Live, I elected to focus on the art of improvisation. Interestingly, Viola Spolin, Paul's mother, developed these games to assist challenged children with their social development.

I decided to incorporate my lighthouse technique into the ten-week session. I had no idea what results to expect. In fact, I experienced anxiety when the administrator explained there would likely be a few teens "carrying." (This was pre-9/11 and security scanners were not a part of our reality.) It was difficult to imagine them being open to improvisation, much less learning a technique that required intense personal scrutiny. As the course progressed and I introduced my Lighthouse Technique, I invited them to consider how they wanted their movie to go.

I will never forget the night, about six weeks into my "experiment" when one of the teens, notoriously aggressive, got stranded and needed a ride home. Being from New York City I don't scare easily but I must confess, I was exceptionally nervous getting in that car alone with him. We rode along for some time in dead silence. Suddenly to my immense surprise he started talking. "So that Lighthouse thing…well I tried it today. This f-ing idiot was on my case and I was about to take him out. Then I stopped for a second and just looked at him and I was like, why bother? I didn't want him in my movie, so I just walked away."

In that moment, I had to strain every molecule to stay cool. It had worked! I had reached him and he now had the power to change his inner dialogue and with that, change *his* story.

How much of our lives do we spend having a dialogue that no longer serves us? Clearly there is no victory, and little joy, in merely surviving. If we want to live a life we love, we must take steps to gain a new vantage point. If we wish to rewrite our story, it begins by being conscious of the words we choose, that ultimately determine who we are being.

LIGHTHOUSE TECHNIQUE—THE 21-DAY CHALLENGE

Begin by rating your movie. Is it an adventure, action-comedy, a drama perhaps? How many stars would you give it? What's the Rotten Tomato rating? Be honest, if you were the studio exec, would it make the cut?

DAY 1 - 7

Spend seven days journaling what you observe from your lighthouse. Do so without judgment. At the end of the week, circle the actions that do not fit how you want your story to go. Then choose one action you see is repetitive and that you no longer want in your repertoire to focus your attention on in the following week.

DAY 8 - 14

Spend the next seven days simply noticing this action. Consider the repercussions of how this action affects you when that scene replays. Continue to observe without judgement. Resist any temptation to belittle yourself. Your job is just to notice. See if you can notice it the moment it begins, or, even better, just before it begins.

DAY 15 - 21

For the remaining 7 days, select a new action, one that serves the story you are authoring, to replace the undesirable one. Every time you notice yourself repeating the action you identified as no longer serving you, see if you can pause and give yourself the opportunity to take your new action.

On day 21, assess your progress and rate your movie again. Has your experience of yourself changed? If so, celebrate, no matter how minor those changes may be. If not, be kind to yourself. Consider how long you have had that old storyline running the show.

REJECT THE OLD MESSAGING

If you take the movie analogy one step further, writing, casting, location hunting, editing all takes time. Yet, when we are in action, committed to authoring our lives, we gain the capacity to take back control of our lives and in so doing, receive high ratings from the toughest critic of all…ourselves.

That said, what will you say to yourself today? How about, "I am…THRIVING!"

ABOUT AMY McKENZIE

Amy's lifetime involvement in the theater offered her many opportunities to study with some of the industry's greatest directors, performers and teachers. Her formal education includes the Master's Program at the American Conservatory Theater in San Francisco and the Film Certificate Program as a Teaching Assistant at UCLA. Her career spans four decades and includes venues from off-Broadway to television, National Tours to Summer Stock. Over the years Miss McKenzie has worked professionally as a producer, director, founding artistic director, writer, actor, professor and coach.

From an early age Amy pursued a passion for personal development, studying a multitude of disciplines from survival techniques to professional leadership training. The degree of her development is evident in her success as a speaker, business owner and transformational coach.

Loving all things natural, Amy has committed a great deal of time to the study of traditional and alternative healing. Miss McKenzie is also a licensed HeartMath practitioner and holds certifications in various alternative healing modalities including Reiki, Energy Restructuring and Rebirthing and as a Therapeutic Masseuse.

Her commitment to furthering the well-being of others is demonstrated by the number of lives she has touched and the contribution she has made as an independent distributor, leader, trainer and presenter for Zija International.

When asked, Amy cites her most cherished accomplishment as having provided significant opportunities for her brilliantly gifted daughter, Valia O'Donnell, to fully live a life she loves.

Making a difference, one person at a time, is Amy's driving force.

THE POWER OF SHARING
by Brenda Hammon

Hi! Let me introduce myself. My name is Brenda Hammon and I'm an entrepreneur at heart.

I've owned several different companies with varying degrees of success over the past 35 years. I've also been an employee, rising to the management level for most of the retail companies I worked for.

I am also a story teller of true life events but that's not how I got started. Let's just say I came from very humble beginning.

My parents earned their living as homesteaders in the early 1950s and work was what they did from sunup to sundown. However, around the age of five years old, I learned there was no one I could count on to keep me safe. The adult son of family friends hired to help on the homestead sexually molested me. Eventually a member of my own family also abused me.

A once outgoing and curious little girl quickly became shy and introverted, hiding in the shadows, watching for any sign of possible danger. Flight and fright was how I survived.

For years, I struggled, trying to make sense of my life and the actions taken by others. Ultimately my own decisions landed me in a very dysfunctional marriage that eventually led to a murder contract on my life.

I married a man I really didn't love but thought was safe and would protect me. Not long after the wedding, all hell broke loose and my new married life turned very ugly, very fast.

Alfred, my new husband, harbored his own dark secrets, secrets that reared their ugly head once we were married. He was possessive and jealous, with a very acute and keen interest in all forms of sadistic sexual fantasies.

Sadly, during our marriage I fell under Alfred's control. With his ever-so-watchful gaze, he knew where I was and where I went all the time. At first, he enlisted the help of spies from my own family. Later, because he didn't work for four years, he took over the "duty."

During his "holiday" from working, I worked three jobs to support our little family but we slowly fell behind. In addition to my three jobs I studied for two years for my Bachelor of Science in Horticulture as well as floral design by correspondence. Before I could finish my Bachelor of Science degree, Alfred put the kibosh on my ability to complete the program because it involved going to another city. Alfred refused to let me leave with our two daughters.

So, with my father's help, I started my own floral business locally. Alfred was right there, "helping me" by keeping tabs on the male customers. The financial pressure that was put on the fledging business led to closing its doors after only four years.

Once again, I felt like an epic failure. I didn't want to face the local townspeople or my family. However, I still had to work to feed my family so, with the shame of defeat as my constant companion, I took a job scrubbing toilets and cleaning rooms in the local motel.

I applaud all chamber maids for the work you do. It's not an easy job and I thank you every time I am at a hotel/motel. I can also tell the rest of you that scrubbing someone else's

33

dirty toilet is a very humbling but therapeutic experience at the same time.

While scrubbing those toilets, I asked myself if this was what I really wanted in my life? If not, then I needed to make some changes if I wanted to survive.

So once more I grabbed my boot straps, pulled myself up and stepped forward.

From there, one of the local Property and Casualty Insurance Offices hired me. I studied and became a Level II General Agent. I enjoyed the challenge of working with nine different companies but after 13 years, reality struck home.

I applied for the Office Manager Job, one I had been doing for several years. With the title came in increase in salary, even though I would be doing exactly what I had been doing for years. However, they hired a new male office manager and I was put in charge of training him on how to do my job. I wasn't even sure how I was supposed to do that because he hadn't yet acquired his General Agent's license. Then, I found out he was getting paid double what I made while running the office. Knowing how they viewed me as a woman disturbed me. I finally understood I would never advance in that male-dominated office.

That realization started me on the path to becoming an entrepreneur.

I decided to go into the Life Insurance business where I knew I could make a difference in people's lives while moving toward becoming my own boss. Once more I hit the books and qualified as a Level II Life and A&S Agent. Looking for a better opportunity, I moved away from my hometown and hit the road, looking for work.

By this time, I felt free to move away because Alfred and I were in the throes of getting a divorce after 21 years. However, he was not a leaving kind of man.

Instead, he aimed to destroy me, believing it would force me to come crawling back to him. When he wasn't stalking me, which included trying to shoot me and my horses, he was phoning my new boss in Edmonton and the President of the company, attempting to get me fired from my job.

As luck would have it, at that point the insurance company converted all life brokers from employees to self-contractors. Alfred lost his leverage on my job security when that happened.

All the power in my life fell back into my own hands. I was no longer terrified the rug would be pulled out from under my feet. My destiny was fully under my control. All I had to do was move forward into the new life waiting for me.

Alfred's sexual obsession led to his early death shortly after our divorce was granted. During the police investigation into his untimely departure, the RCMP searched his computer and found he had hired someone to kill me.

Talk about knocking one's socks off with that news! I was in shock and once again running for my life but this time from an unknown attacker.

However, it all ended well. As you can tell I'm alive and kicking and writing about this journey. I'm happy to report my husband, Bud has my back.

After a few stops and starts, I've now been my own boss for nearly 15 years. Our life insurance company, Spirit Creek Financial has flourished. I'm one of the top producers in Canada in the companies I deal with and on the National Advisory Board for one for the Leading Lifestyle Protection Companies in Canada since its inception about six years ago.

I enjoy helping people figure out their financial needs if something terrible like death or disability should happen to their family before they acquire their wealth. I'm the agent in the trenches. While my clients plan their futures, I make sure that, if things should go wrong, the survivors are looked after.

Because the life insurance business can be lonely for the independent agent, I started Spirit Creek Financial, MGA (Mentor, Guide, Assist) to help other life agents through product training and showing them how to attain their dreams in this business.

However, with all my success, something was still missing. The urge to help other women like myself kept pulling at me. I wanted to make something positive out of all the chaos of my past so I decided to write and self-publish my story and share how I overcame the odds.

Spirit Creek Publishing developed from that seed. It started as a platform to market my own books but soon self-published books by others will grace the website.

Self-publishing and sharing my story about sexual abuse, incest, physical, mental and emotional abuse has been both terrifying and rewarding. Standing on the stage and inspiring other women from all walks of life and experiences is truly an honor. I feel humbled and grateful to be able to reach out and help those who have been traumatized because of their past.

I was called a philanthropist by Jo Dibblee one day and it surprised me to be placed in that category. I never really thought about it like that when I donated my books to women's shelters. I simply wanted to reach those women because it seemed the likelihood of them attending an event to hear me speak was remote. Sending my books to the women who live in those communities is one way of helping others.

Because of my past, I can stand tall and be the voice for the thousands and thousands of women (and men) who have no voice. I am an ordinary woman, who decided my past was not going to define me and my abusers were not going to destroy me.

So how does this story about my past relate to business and being a successful business person? Three words: Perseverance. Determination. Focus. You need those three things to survive anything in life, love and business.

I can confidently say my past made me stronger, determined and resistant. I know for a fact nothing can stop me from following my dreams, no matter how crazy and far-fetched they may be.

I'm grateful to my past, the trials and tribulations made me, a confidante, self-aware, empathic, understanding woman with a wicked sense of humor.

May all of us live the life we were meant to live in our business, love and life!

As Thoreau said, "Go confidently in the direction of your dreams. Live the life you've imagined."

REJECT THE OLD MESSAGING

37

ABOUT BRENDA HAMMON

Brenda Hammon resides in Alberta Beach in Alberta with her spouse William (Bud) Portwood, numerous horses, two dogs and one cat, plus a few strays that come around. Brenda enjoys riding her horse Hughie, building things (nothing too small) like barns and sheds and spending time with their children and grandchildren.

Brenda found her passion for writing after she wrote her first book about her early life and continues to write and share her story with speaking to groups and writing about subjects that no one wants to discuss openly. Brenda is twice an international best-selling author with her books.

Brenda also has a successful life insurance business with her husband Bud and together they mentor other independent agents to be their best in their chosen field. She has served on the National Advisory Board for one of the Leading Lifestyle Protection Companies in Canada since its inception and actively shares her ideas and views of what the everyday client is looking for with the company.

Brenda finds satisfaction sharing her knowledge and expertise with any organization that requires her help. Not one to back away from a challenge, Brenda (though not that fond of flying) even jumped out of an airplane at 14,000 feet to raise money for a local charity that helps victimized women find safety.

A few of Brenda's strengths include determination, focus, perseverance, compassion and empathy. Her two mottos in life are: "Go big or Go home" and "How hard can it be?" And she applies them to everything she does in life.

Brenda believes that if you work hard enough you can achieve anything. She's grateful for her decision to move beyond her past to build the life she wants.

YOU'RE NOT FINISHED
by Teresa Syms

"You're not finished here yet!"

Those words have been whispered into my mind and soul many times throughout my life. I really had no idea what they meant, why I kept hearing them, or who was speaking to me.

The first time those words were committed to my mind, I was in my late teens, struggling with everything life had thrown at me. You see, I was born crippled into an extremely dysfunctional family.

An abusive, mean alcoholic, my father was extremely frustrated with his life. During my childhood, when I misbehaved, he forced me to kneel on beer caps nailed to a piece of plywood, pointed side up. If I slouched, he strapped me with a leather belt. Every time he forced me onto this board, I was placed in front of a full-length mirror to add to the torture. It was here I learned self-loathing and began hating myself and my existence.

My mother was what I call the 3D's: deaf, depressed and delusional. She took pleasure in telling me I wasn't wanted and was nothing but a problem to her. She also took great pleasure watching my father wreak her vengeance on me because she made him dish out the punishment. It was his penance because he had wanted another child and she didn't. I was the result and due to the extra time and care needed to straighten my legs, my mother resented me and the disruption my condition caused the family.

My older sister was jealous, insecure and hateful. She took great pains to create the incidents for which I was punished. Every day saw a new adventure in torture. She hit me, humiliated me, called me disgusting names and forced me to leave the house for school every day cold, hungry and with nothing to eat for the day. This caused me to grow up with an eating disorder I was unaware of until my children asked why I only ate one meal per day.

This was the home I grew up in: unloved, unwanted, hungry and angry.

My mother convinced our family doctor to put me on tranquilizers for depression, and in keeping with family tradition, I began drinking heavily at age 14. By the time I was 17, my life felt like an unbearable disaster.

In addition, my mother had no idea the doctor was sexually assaulting me during my office visits. I remained silent because there really was no one to tell. No one would believe a kid! The combination of medication and alcohol helped numb my pain but the anguish and loneliness I felt consumed me daily.

I was alone in this world. My boyfriend left after I gave up my friends for him and our relationship. High school was useless to me, so I left in grade eleven and tried to make it on my own. Angry, I lashed out at everyone who came near me.

One night, I reached my limit and got behind the wheel of my father's car. I knew exactly the tree that would help me end this miserable existence. Off I drove in a drunken, drugged haze.

On a cold, dark night in January, no one else was on the country road. "'My" tree loomed in the distance and I accelerated towards it. My grip tightened on the steering wheel.

This was it! At last, my pain would finally end.

Never more determined in my life, I raced towards the tree.

Then suddenly...my mind went blank. Hyperaware of my surroundings, time seemed to stand still and the silence was deafening. Seconds before the impact, the steering wheel wrenched from my hands and, to my surprise, I was back on the road and slowing down.

That was when I first heard, "YOU'RE NOT FINISHED HERE YET!"

With tears streaming down my face, I stopped the car and looked around. I was alone in my shocked, stunned, silence. What had happened and who spoke to me? I turned the interior lights on expecting to see someone in the back seat but there was no one there!

I didn't understand what had happened.

Driving home and going to bed I at first thought I imagined the entire incident. But I knew I hadn't! Someone or something stopped me from killing myself. I prayed as I went to sleep and in that moment, I became aware of my Guardian Angel.

As my life moved forward, I thought marriage and having children would ease my soul. And it would have, had I married the right person for the right reasons.

In life, we are what we know and that's how I began my marriage. The abuse was physical at first. Then, after my nose had to be rebuilt, he turned to emotional and psychological abuse.

Twenty-five years in this situation left me emotionally alone, living with people who teased me, corrected me constantly, ignored me and laughed at me.

REJECT THE OLD MESSAGING

Once again, I found myself locked deep down in a black pit of despair.

Being raised Catholic, I found peace and solace by sitting quietly in the church. One afternoon, as I sat in silent contemplation and prayer, hoping to find an answer as to why I was being tested so harshly, I raised my eyes up to the figure on the cross.

Suddenly, tears began to pour down my face and my heart felt like it would explode! As I stared at the statue, the face turned and looked directly at me. In disbelief, I blinked hard several times. No, it was still looking at me. Turning away, I looked at the statue of Mary to find she also was looking directly at me.

Then I heard it again..." YOU'RE NOT FINISHED HERE YET."

Why did I keep hearing these words? Who was saying them? What did they mean for me? The pain in my heart eased and I found renewed strength and courage. I went home, thinking things would be better.

I soon discovered this was the beginning of another end.

When my grandmother, who was also my godmother, turned eighty years old, her health declined rapidly but her children refused to take care of her. I took my grandmother into my own home and my children and I cared for her. I bathed her, we read to her and did all we could to show her how much she was loved and wanted.

After a few years in my home, she began feeling uncomfortable around my husband, and chose to move to a retirement home. An incredibly strong woman who had been sold off as a child because her step-father got her pregnant, she keenly felt the loss of her independence and wanted to die.

Then, in 2003, at the age of 91, my grandmother fell seriously ill. At that time, my children were almost grown and heading off to school. They no longer needed me and I felt abandoned in my marriage. I found the courage and strength to act on the plans I made three years earlier to venture out on my own.

I took the lowest of jobs just to earn my own money and obtain a credit rating as a single person. My doctor at that time helped me as much as possible through my separation, divorce and my grandmother's illness.

To compound the situation, an older man at work made me his target for sexual harassment. Because he was respected by the owners, I felt I had nowhere to turn. One day my anxiety became so great, I lost my eyesight for twenty minutes at work. Fear overwhelmed me and I made mistakes constantly.

Finally, one Saturday, as we were in the midst of dividing up our 25-year marital property, a call came from the nursing home. My grandmother had died in her sleep. It felt like the last person on this earth who cared about me was gone. When I entered her room later that morning, I lay my head on her unmoving chest and cried from the depths of my soul.

As her Power of Attorney and Executrix, but moving in a complete fog, I fulfilled my duties to my grandmother. Through her help, I finally had some money to start out on my own at 43.

Taking back my life was the best thing I ever did. I enjoyed my independence and went to college for the first time. I met a great man, who not only supported me throughout this difficult time, but I knew he was my soul mate. Together we are unstoppable!

In 2005, I moved from Brantford to London to help raise his sons. I graduated from college with honours in Human Resources and Business. I even landed the job I wanted before I graduated. Life was great!

In 2006, Don and I married and began our new life together.

Eight months later, on a bitter cold February afternoon during an ice storm, I got into my Dodge Ram and headed home, changing my route because of the storm. Another pickup truck heading towards me spun out of control. Everyone on that road stopped to give this driver room. On and off the road they swerved and spun as they fought to regain control.

Time stood still as I watched, waited, and braced myself. With a death-grip on the steering wheel, foot pushed into the brake pedal, I thought, "I will never see my husband or children again."

A second in time is all it takes to change a life, end a life or begin a life.

As I watched that truck spin just feet in front of me, I believed I was going to die. In the moment before the crash, I heard those words again.

"YOU'RE NOT FINISHED HERE YET!"

For the next five years, I battled with non-visible injuries including soft-tissue and muscle damage, severe whiplash, fractured teeth, sprained wrists, ankles, knee and damaged hip. But the worst injury was the brain trauma. It caused vertigo, speech difficulties, memory problems and loss of balance. Seven times I fell down the stairs, resulting in several more disc herniations.

For five years, I struggled to regain my health. I battled with insurance companies, lawyers, doctors and many other so-called rehabilitation professionals. My life was discussed openly, and nothing was private, as I lived under surveillance. However, to me, the worst part was having a dollar value attached to my life.

Ten years after the accident, when I was finally left alone and could once again focus on my life, I attempted going back to work and failed miserably. My injuries made me understand in no uncertain terms that they are with me for the long haul.

I needed another way, but what? Giving up was no longer an option.

I took courses on self-improvement and sought professional help to help me deal with my past traumas. I worked part-time from home but in my heart, I knew I had a bigger purpose.

"YOU'RE NOT FINISHED HERE YET!"

It was finally making sense.

Since my two lifelong passions were writing and helping other people I used writing as a form of healing. I began by writing about my grandmother's life, thinking this was my purpose. That eventually changed into writing about how personal identity and deep-seated family secrets have long lasting and devastating effects on future generations.

YES! This was it.

For months I wrote, rewrote, edited, and ignored my health until finally, my book was finished. I felt exhausted but free. For the first time in my life, the past had no hold on me. I forgave my family for the abuse, trauma and neglect I was raised with.

Finally, I understand what those words mean. "YOU'RE NOT FINISHED HERE YET!"

As part of my growth and the need to break free from a life of trauma, I embarked on courses such as Shame and Vulnerability by Brené Brown. I dug deep and found my strength and purpose once again. I trusted the process and became a Personal Empowering Coach and author. Today, I champion women who have experienced trauma or abuse. I show them how to break their silence and step into a future filled with courage and strength.

I can say with certainty that no matter what life may have thrown at you, you can be a strong, independent woman by conquering one limiting belief at a time. Through visualizations and setting new, powerful intentions for your life, you can use whatever your past taught you and learn from it. Negative experiences don't have to own you or define you. Use them as your personal life lessons to inspire others. As a business woman, your success creates a platform that lets you extend your reach.

I truly believe, "I'M NOT FINISHED HERE YET!" Are you?

ABOUT TERESA SYMS

Born crippled, Teresa was a fighter from the beginning. She survived a childhood filled with abuse, and after attempting vehicular suicide, she became aware of divine intervention.

"You're Not Finished Here Yet," she heard.

Trying to escape her past, but unaware of the depth of her emotional scars, she married and started a family, which years later ended in divorce. Later, she remarried and went to college to begin a career in Human Resources. Eight months later she faced death head on. Dealing with chronic injuries, Teresa gave up for nine years.

Then she stood up and rebuilt her life. Entrepreneurship became her calling. Today, Teresa leads a life filled with limitless possibilities with her husband, Don, and her Bouvier des Flanders puppy, Axel.

Along with her new book, *A Century of Secrets*, Teresa hosts her own radio show, Powering Through Life, which you can listen to at TeresaSyms.com. She is also the owner of Sterling Silver Coaching, focusing on personal empowerment for women.

Teresa is living proof that through courage and determination you can give yourself a brilliant future.

THE POWER OF THE DOMINATRIX
by Dana Pharant

"You're stupid!"

"You can't do that you're a girl!"

"You would be pretty if you just lost that extra weight!"

I know these statements all too well. In fact, I heard these judgments so often and in so many variations that by the time I left home, I believed all of it. After all, it must be true when I heard it over and over, right?

I had no idea I had the right to question these warped perceptions of me or reject them altogether. I didn't know I could believe something different.

Here's the thing: I grew up in a cult, brainwashed day in and day out that being female meant you were less than a man. Top that off with an emotionally unavailable father and a narcissistic step-mother and you get a deadly combination for eroding self esteem.

My self-image was based on utter lies.

I wasn't stupid. In fact, my intelligence is measured in the top 3-5% of the population yet I bought that twisted perception pushed on me.

I wasn't ugly or fat. Looking back, I see a stunning young woman who carried maybe twenty extra pounds—just enough to create lovely soft curves. Yet I bought into the idea I wasn't lovable because I wasn't a size 8.

I won't bore you with the details of what one does when they believe they are unlovable, stupid or unattractive. I'm sure you can fill in those blanks well enough. I would even hazard a guess you may have engaged in some version of your own self-destructive behaviours.

What's important about my story is that those 'other-imposed' ideas started my journey of self discovery. Moving through various therapies, healing tools, self help books and seminars I searched to find THE answer. I wanted to feel whole again, to fill the void I thought was missing from my body and soul.

I attended therapy sessions where I beat on pillows and let out primal screams that would make your toes curl, hoping to release the rage so neatly hidden under the fear and the pain.

I went for Reiki sessions, looking to realign my soul to it's higher purpose, hoping to feel I belonged on this crazy planet.

I tried 'clean' eating to purge out the negativity and toxins in my body, looking for spiritual enlightenment to ease the aching in my soul.

They were all fun and yes, they all helped somewhat but the foundational lie remained. The one that said I was somehow broken. Until I came to grips with that lie and my belief in it, nothing I tried for "fixing" me was ever going to be good enough.

Then one day I stumbled on this concept: Who I really am is an Infinite Being. No one and nothing is more powerful than me.

This struck a chord deep down inside, shaking the very foundation I had believed was true. As the shaking continued, it loosened the hold the old lies and beliefs had on me.

As an Infinite Being, all this crap I carried around was irrelevant and unnecessary.

Now, I'm not going to blow smoke up your arse and tell you I instantly stepped out of the crap and into the magical place of sunshine and rainbows. Ha! Not quite!

It did, however, dramatically speed up my process of dropping those crazy beliefs and self judgments. It allowed me to re-connect with who I truly am at my core. It created an ever-expanding and deepening of the connection with self and the Universe at large.

I continued to go to workshops and seminars, with one dramatic difference: I stopped going because there was something to fix, and instead had fun with the tools. I no longer NEEDED to go; I WANTED to go!

I longed to break free of more limitations. I loved playing with the energy and what it could do. This exponentially increased the effect of the things I learned.

As I attended, I watched others struggle to get things to work. I could see they constantly wondered why the same problem (often lack of money or weight issues) kept cropping up, despite taking all the classes specifically for that issue.

I realized that underneath it all was this belief they were broken, and even though they heard the same concept "You're an infinite being," nothing changed at their core. It seemed to me the people running those workshops and courses skipped over that concept, not giving it the time and attention I saw it needed so people could embody it.

I decided to change the game and take a fresh approach by sharing the real key. I wasn't there to just sell courses over and over.

These days, showing clients they aren't broken delights me. I watch as their loop of problems crumbles and falls away. They step into who they really are—an infinite being! One who is beautiful, powerful and brilliant!

Getting people to this incredible space lies at the heart of my work. They no longer NEED me. Rather, they choose to work with me because it's fun and expands their lives and their businesses.

This understanding of being an infinite being is also behind my choice to utilise my experience as a Dominatrix as a metaphor in my coaching work.

The Dominatrix embodies the energy of that strong confident female who refuses to see herself as broken or needing to be fixed. She allows herself to receive the praise and adoration of her followers. Her quiet and unapologetic strength magnetically attracts her clients. There is no need to bully people to work with her as she has her pick of clients and takes only a select few who are the right fit.

You don't need to become a Dominatrix to embody this energy. Rather, she is an archetype for us to learn from, a role model. She guides us to step out and take bold action in our businesses and for the sake of our customers and clients.

Accepting there is nothing wrong with you is also invaluable to your business. There are bound to be mistakes and things that don't turn out quite the way we envisioned. I know this all too well. I have been in business for 25+ years and let me tell you, I've had my fair share of f-ups.

The Dominatrix shows us that when we make a mistake we simply correct it without drawing attention to it. The last thing anyone wants to hear from the Dominatrix is "oops." It throws off the whole scene and takes you out of the sweet delicious surrender you were enjoying. So, knowing that "oops" is a disservice to her clients she ignores the mistake and moves on quickly, taking charge of the situation with ease.

Time spent beating yourself up, or feeling ashamed about what happened is counterproductive. Learn from the results and use that same time to move your business forward instead.

We do well to emulate the Dominatrix in business, to take swift action to course correct when needed. We may need to train ourselves to pull this off automatically but the rewards are well worth the effort.

One of the other valuable business tools I discovered in my journey is the concept of expanding out. Typically, people who teach energy work train you to shield or bubble yourself from others. While I found this helpful (and it was a lifesaver at the time), it never seemed to prevent me from being a sponge to everyone else's energy. I had to employ time-consuming cleansing rituals and go for energy sessions to remove the residue I carried.

I am all about finding easier solutions so I kept digging until I uncovered something to keep me my energy clear and required minimal effort to keep in place: the concept of "expanding out."

From an energy perspective, the more we expand our energy out (even to the size of the Universe or beyond) the easier it becomes to break free of taking on other people's thoughts, emotions, or energies as our own. This practice allows us to separate from those things we mistakenly label as ours that belong to someone else.

From a business perspective, this tool helps you to let go of negative feedback and other blocks to your success. It's also fantastic for tapping into the wisdom of the "Infinite," also called Source or God. When you expand out, you lower your resistance to this wisdom and open up to receive the knowledge waiting for you.

In respect to your business, consider the difference it would make if you were directly plugged in. What would it mean to access your intuition and follow it? After all, has your gut feeling ever been wrong?

Intuition works at the speed of light, while your brain works at the speed of a race car. Which would you rather harness?

So, here's your assignment—should you choose to accept it.

Create an alarm on your phone with a distinct but gentle sound (like ocean waves), that goes off every 30 min. When you hear that sound, take 1 or 2 deep breaths and let your energy expand out to the size of the Universe. This starts the retraining necessary to let go of those false beliefs and move into owning your brilliance.

REJECT THE OLD MESSAGING

ABOUT DANA PHARANT

Dana lives with her amazingly supportive husband in Barrie, Ontario. She loves to cook for friends and sharing a fabulous bottle of wine. She has been nicknamed the "wine snob," and could have become a sommelier.

Her work is her passion although side hobbies include getting out on the motorbike for a tour across the countryside. That often includes stopping to discover a new pub with incredible food. Being more of an introvert, she loves relaxing in the backyard or having a laugh with an intimate group of friends.

Dana has worked with clients for the past 25 years and earned the title of Master Healer, pulling in a wide range of physical bodywork training, energy therapy training, and emotional/psychotherapy training. Add in her highly sensitive intuition and she brings a range of tools and skills to her work few others can match.

Having built and run a million-dollar business with all the ups and downs associated with it, she has strong business skills. By harnessing her background as a Dominatrix, she helps entrepreneurs claim their Inner Dominatrix so they rock their business and live bold, sexy, fun-filled lives.

STEP TWO

THE *Power* OF BEING YOURSELF

You can't please everyone,
and you can't make everyone like you.
~ Katie Couric ~

BE YOURSELF
by Erin Best

When Candace and I did our original interview on Divas That Care, I was just starting out. Fast forward to now and I'm chugging along with a much different outlook. My core principles are the same since I began my real estate business but through personal growth, development and of course, work experience, my focus has shifted. I've also learned some powerful lessons.

I always prided myself on my gift to build relationships and network, a talent for listening, the ability to get things done and a positive outlook—those sorts of things. I'm harnessing the best traits of my personality but also tending to traits that needed developing.

Now, almost three years into a growing business, I'm focused more on being AUTHENTIC. I see my world as a garden now. I plant business and grow my client base but it's so much more than that.

It's the HOW and WHY behind it. HOW and WHY am I generating my business? HOW and WHY am I maintaining my client base and growing it?

I said my world is a garden now and it's true. I recently started a Real Estate Coaching program complete with amazing tools to help generate and grow my business. I personally experienced the benefits of these tools and witnessed the growth of my peers in the program from using them. But for me, something was missing, like personal puzzle pieces I needed in order to realize the full potential of the program.

I recently read a post on Facebook that summed it up for me:

"The obligation for working mothers is a very precise one: the feeling that one ought to work as if one did not have children, while raising one's children as if one did not have a job."

Is it any wonder my business and life felt like a roller coaster? It's why I felt sub-par in every role I tried to fulfill from motherhood to business woman to wife, to friend. It's why I questioned myself when prospective clients went with someone else to represent them in their real estate transactions. I felt I needed to implement everything I was learning in the coaching program but also felt I was failing at the same time.

I had no idea where to start, how to execute and how to follow up or follow through.

So, I took a step back. On a call with my coach, we searched for that missing piece until I realized I never felt quite "good enough."

A shift happened on our coaching call that day. We decided it was time to take "Erin the Judge" out of my world.

She was no longer allowed to dwell on things I should have done differently. She was no longer allowed to make me feel like a failure every time I yelled at my kids because I felt frustrated about my husband being away at work or for not landing a new listing I thought was a home run. She was no longer allowed to judge my behavior for ANYTHING.

In fact, I took the word "should" right out of my vocabulary. Letting go wasn't easy at first but what happened over the course of the next six weeks was magic. (And I'm not exaggerating how quickly the change happened!)

I still work on not judging every single action every day. It is still hard but I make conscience efforts.

What I feel now is this: Free. Happy.

My relationships changed, including my relationship with my husband. Our weekends together shifted to happy experiences and laughter. Now we WANT to spend time together instead of "alone time" to decompress from a busy week. We look forward all week to the weekend because we enjoy each other's company so much.

I am also a happier mom to my kids. They no longer feel like they are "in my way" on my rise to the top. In fact, they motivate me to get things done so I can spend more time with them.

Even my relationship with myself improved. If I leave something to do tomorrow, that's okay, because I stopped telling myself I "should have" done it the night before when I was exhausted.

Changes in my business occurred, as well. My focused shifted back to the basics of meeting and EXCEEDING client expectations. I now land more listings and convert cold prospects into warm clients who I look forward to chatting with. I concentrate on the activities that make clients and prospective clients go, "WOW. She's pretty awesome."

Today, as I write this, was one of those days. While calling a mobile park unit for clients I discovered some critical information that affected their decision to purchase in that community. Rather than seeing this hiccup as a mild annoyance, I served my clients instead.

It transformed my whole day.

I no longer feel I have to "fake it till I make it." I am already there. I just need to "till my garden" (that garden metaphor again). I am busy "weeding" my garden, "fertilizing" my garden, "tilling" my garden so as I plant the seeds of growth, my garden will be lush.

That sounds really nice to me.

So, while many others in our coaching group execute things to generate business, my time is better spent becoming a better version of myself; one that is more caring, more nurturing but most importantly, more forgiving.

I am who I am.

It is a lesson I am grateful for. While I appreciate and believe there is a place for "faking it 'till you're making it," there is an even bigger place for being authentic and taking ownership over who you are as a person. By understanding ourselves and our own personality traits, we also learn a tremendous amount about the people we interact with.

So often we hear about "conflicting personality types." Which is real, but if you have a greater understanding of yourself, can you not understand others better? Of course, you can!

In learning who we are, we better serve our relationships. It becomes a wonderful thing.

Have I mastered that art? No. It's a work in progress because there are no more "shoulds" in my life.

By learning who I am, cherishing my positive traits and harnessing the "electricity" in my personality, I now deliver a better quality of relationship to those I encounter, both in my business and personal spheres.

I've shifted who I associate myself with, as well. I'm not sure if it was ever a conscious choice but changing who I choose to spend time with has been beneficial. Kind of like those success articles suggesting you "dress for success." It's the same for the company you keep.

I met a world-class videographer I teamed with for some listings this year. His positive energy creates more positive energy. My Real Estate Coach has been a tremendous influence on me and my belief that my goals are completely attainable in a fairly short period of time. He is a good fit for me, as he knows "how" to coach me to be productive and positive.

Earlier this year, my good friend Nicole Rice, owner of an online boutique shop called Sweet {Jolie}, started a campaign to "Love Yourself." While I did not submit anything to her, the question she asked resonated with me.

"What would you tell your teen or younger self?"

This was poignant to me because in my tween years I was grossly insecure. Not cool enough to be friends with the "cool crowd," I didn't feel I fit in with the other "crowds" either. I was lost somewhere in between.

Not sure of how to act or who I was, I swam competitively. Swimming was a world where I felt happy and comfortable. It was authentic to me, the right garden to be working in, if you will.

Today, I would tell my teen self that the best is yet to come. You will make silly mistakes and some mistakes you will wish you could take back. Some mistakes will cost you friendships along the way, but that's a part of growing up and it's okay to let them go.

I would also tell my teen self that even the adults we respect and admire sometimes do not have all the answers. I'd tell her you will have to put some demons to bed and you will have to love yourself first to attract your tribe…but they will come. They will be there to support you and listen to you and they will have your back.

As an extrovert, I have many acquaintances, friends and colleagues but my true tribe is a smaller circle of individuals. These are the people with whom I can share what's on my mind and they do not try to wrap a "silver lining" around me.

They are the people who say, "Lean on me, girl. I know you're having a rough time and I'm not going to judge. I'm going to just let you feel what you're feeling." These people are my people. The people who do not make me feel bad for feeling bad or some other emotion other than "thankful." Because everyone has a bad day, right?

These are the people you want to align yourself with. The people who work for their success and can teach you while being honest with you. I want friends who would risk hurting my feelings for the truth rather than fib to protect my feelings. Honest, hard-working, fun loving, ambitious people of integrity.

Coming full circle, I realize the value I admire most in people comes down to this one quality.

Authenticity.

Authenticity seeds harvests like honesty, integrity, and positivity. It creates this magnetic energy you simply cannot resist.

I guess you could say my focus for this chapter was "Learn enough about yourself to be as authentic as you can." It's where positive change begins. Real and lasting change in the world around us starts small, like a seed in the garden. We water and nurture that seed by embracing our uniqueness from the inside out.

Once you start your own journey of self-exploration and self-love, you will notice this wonderful flow from being yourself. It's kind of like nurturing your soul.

You'll drop the "shoulds" and not care so much about what anyone else thinks about you. Your success will be determined by your mindset and how you react to situations. You will get "lucky" if you follow your heart and get out of your head. You will surrender so you can enjoy your life and actually live it.

BUSINESS DIVAS THAT CARE

The example we set for our children and friends starts the ripple of change. Embracing who we are from the inside out gives those around us permission to use their gifts to create their own positive change.

Life does not have to be so hard. Sometimes you need to take a step back from the hard work you have been putting in to see the garden of your life in a different light.

To see it authentically.

ABOUT ERIN BEST

Erin lives in St. Albert, Alberta with her husband Paul O'Connor and two children, Sean and Harper. Her extended family is spread throughout Alberta, Ontario and Nova Scotia. She enjoys travelling with her family, patio pints with her husband, sushi dates with her son and stroller walks with her daughter. She practices Real Estate as a licensed REALTOR® with Realty Executives Masters in the Greater Edmonton Area.

FROM THE HEART
by Camille Bowling

I had the good fortune of working from a young age, learning what it was like to earn my own money. My father was the sole breadwinner in our home while my mom stayed home with the kids. Today I am grateful for my childhood and the skills my parents taught me. They were always supported my decisions so when I ventured out on my own in 1978 to open my own hair salon they were 100% behind me.

It was the best decision I ever made.

For me the time freedom and tax savings were huge. Over the years, I taught my clients the benefits of a home-based business and directed them to many books they often passed on to others.

I have the unique ability to help others make decisions and move forward in both their personal and business lives. It gives me great joy looking back on friends and clients living their passion because of conversations we had years earlier! Although I'm not a trained business coach or counsellor, I trust my inherent natural skills and inner gifts and speak from my heart.

I learned that trust in an interesting way.

My career as a hair dresser meant I was always standing behind my customers, speaking to a mirror. If there was a point to be made or someone pointed a finger at me it felt okay because I was always speaking to a reflection. That distance made it easy for me to deflect and avoid. I'm sure if I asked other hairdressers they'd say they all do it and aren't even aware of the distance it places between them and the other person.

Then one day a client accused me of being selfish because I wasn't having children. It shocked me so much I came around to speak to her face-to-face without the buffer of the mirror. I think it was the first time I looked someone directly in the eye and took in the whole of them. That shift helped me speak from my heart.

Since then I've become more cognizant of looking at people. I think it's important because I know when I'm speaking to someone and they're looking all over the place it drives me crazy. I want them to see ME, to connect with me as a person.

To me, the mirror is a metaphor for the way we create "safe zones" between us, especially these days. Person to person connection is becoming a rare thing.

I am an intuit and a healer. I'm very aware of the energy between us. Before society recognized and accepted energy work, I was called a "voodoo wacko devil woman."

It was up to me to accept the value of what I did. Then I had to step away from the mirror and connect with people so they felt the impact of a heart connection.

These days, it's even more of a challenge to create those connections. As good as the internet is, it has also dramatically shifted us as people. There are a lot of changes brought about by the wired world, not all of them positives. Social media has taught us being genuine can get us into scary places but being genuine works between people.

Face to face connection adds a depth missing in the mirror world of social media. It's easy to hide and deflect, to only show what we want them to see. To be ourselves openly and honestly takes courage.

We must use our God-given intuition and set aside everyone else's opinion about us. I know who I am and I know what people say. Acknowledging the power of what I do often moves me to tears.

Writing this chapter was difficult. I can't say I didn't work hard on it but I also knew I wasn't quite getting what was needed for this book. At one point, I almost called and backed out but I didn't want to quit. I knew the writing would pull me through some difficult places but I wanted to reach out to you.

The experience was good but it wasn't easy. I began to question myself. I don't have a website. I don't have a presence on the internet. I'm not a qualified this or a qualified that so I beat myself up for a bit.

Finally, I asked myself what I was doing this for? WHO was I doing this for? What was the impact I wanted my chapter to have?

Those questions helped me get clear on my message. They are also the questions you need to ask yourself about your business.

As for me, I want women to own their power to connect. I want them to understand how powerful they are without comparing themselves to others. There have been many lessons I've learned along the way but I think the most challenging and difficult one is summed up in this quote: "*It's none of my business what you think of me.*"

The world is waiting for women to get out of the grasp of those things holding them back and share the power of being genuine. My Grandma taught me one of my most important truths. "*Always continue to learn to be a better person.*"

Become a student of daily personal development.

Whether it is reading, listening to tapes, meditating or taking a walk, when I dedicate time in my day for myself I achieve far more. The same power is available to you.

How does this help us succeed in business? Often, when we think we must "sell" we freeze up. We may start out with enthusiasm and passion and then we turn on the computer. We compare ourselves to the "gurus" we encounter there. We start to second guess and it seems like a switch flips somewhere inside of us. Suddenly we take on a persona that's not us. We speak to "the mirror" and then wonder why people become suspicious and avoid us.

Our customer wants us to look them in the eye and be genuine, not a reflection of who we think we should be. Too often we wait to get it all right before we move forward. We become so afraid of making a mistake, we freeze.

Take a risk. Be you!

Stop judging yourself, get out of the mirror zone and connect with people in a real way to succeed. The power of being ourselves removes the "icky thing" keeping us from our economic independence. Come from the heart and everything becomes easier.

The other piece of this puzzle is believing it's okay to create an income for yourself. After all, don't you want an income from your business? Financial stress is the biggest illness in the world.

Without sales, there is no business. Begin by letting of the idea you must be pushy to sell. Selling is about offering something of value to your client and answering their questions. Everything changes when you finally understand your customer has a problem or need and you have the solution they're looking for.

The power of owning yourself, knowing who YOU are and that what you offer has value, lets you make a connection with others from a sense of service. When you're strong in this belief, you project value "out there" and your customer feels it. But when you try to maintain a façade, you can't offer value because you're too busy keeping that mirror in place.

For me, coming out from behind the mirror that day took courage to connect in a way that was genuine and served us both. It's about trusting and believing that when you face the other person you are still your own person and can be of service.

To be the change I want to see, I don't need to speak to the world. Rather, I prefer to reach one person at a time and show them the value of networking and connection. My goal is to help you enlarge your reach. When you make a bigger difference, we've both had an impact.

Reach out to your tribe. Being self-employed for 39 years, I know asking for help isn't easy but find someone who believes in you and won't buy into your crap. Running your own business can be scary and can bring up all your fears about failure.

North American society values extraversion and supports the myth of the independent success. We're taught to admire the person who pulls herself up by the bootstraps. As business women, we're believe that somehow, we should be able to do this ourselves but that's a crock.

We have no problem giving someone else good advice but often we don't even listen to ourselves. It helps to step outside yourself and have someone mirror your advice back to you.

I love working with entrepreneurs and small business owners who understand they can't do it all themselves and seek help in reaching their goals. I work together one-on-one with other women using strategies to ensure their success as they build their own business.

THE POWER OF BEING YOURSELF

I believe there's a change coming. We're hungry for real connection. That's why Snapchat and Facebook Live are so powerful because we're at least seeing people again. It changes the conversation completely. Even the phone changes things. Meet their eyes. Its why more and more people are turning to tools like Skype and Zoom. And there's nothing wrong with those tools as long as they don't get in the way of connecting to people on a genuine level.

I was born at the end of the baby boomer generation, feeling extremely grateful to be living in a healthy body. I received a shock recently when Hubby pointed out that soon I would receive CPP. Now more than ever, I believe "age is only a number!"

Before I go to sleep I meditate on this quote by Mahatma Gandhi. *"Be the change that you want to see in the world."* Then I review my day and give gratitude for five things in my life.

There are two ways to look at life: I can be miserable or I can inspire others. Whatever must be done, it always comes down to a choice. It just takes a willingness to begin. People want to be led well. They want to know their future is in safe hands and to have assurance that their best interests are important. They need to believe their leaders make sound, effective decisions.

So, step into your greatness and find the true essence of the gifts you possess. Become the magnetic and powerful woman you need to be to sustain YOU! Become a woman capable of influencing others to be their best by being yourself. Find your dreams, your passions and your purpose. By taking hold of them as though your last breath depends on it will give you the energy you need to go on.

See people for who they are. Stop talking to the mirror. Connect.

ABOUT CAMILLE BOWLING

Camille Bowling grew up in a family of six in a small farming community on the Lower Mainland of BC. She feels blessed to have had loving parents and an extended family as a part of her life. She's been happily married to her best friend and soul mate, Ross for close to 30 years and everyday feels grateful for the life they share.

She worked many jobs throughout her youth, then, in 1978, after completing a hairdressing apprenticeship, she opened her own home-based hair salon. It's a decision she never regretted.

Ten years later, she started a second career as a marketing entrepreneur. Helping people realize their dreams inspires her to this day.

Camille has enjoyed leadership roles in many organizations. Each experience prepared her for the next endeavor. As a student of personal development, she still has to remind herself to dedicate "ME" time in her day.

Her wish for every woman is to remember to "Love thyself the way you are!"

STEP THREE

Harness

THE POWER OF PASSION

Knowing what must be done does away with fear.
~ Rosa Parks ~

HOW TO FIND YOUR WHY
by Tammy Boucher

I dreamt of being an entrepreneur since the tender age of 5. No kidding.

Like most kids, my first venture was a lemonade stand. Without even realizing I was doing it, I treated it like a business. I tracked the cups and the lemonade and my mom and sister helped me write it all down.

In a way, I did my own bookkeeping at the age of 6.

The following year I noticed a big trend in popsicles. All the kids were buying them so off I went to the mom and pop store on the corner and asked if I could front popsicle sticks. The owner made a deal with me. "I'll sell you these at this price and next week you need to pay for them."

At that age, I looked like Shirley Temple. Blue eyes. Blonde hair with pigtails. That was me.

I wasn't afraid to go door to door at all. In fact, it was fun for me. Mom would get so worried when I was little thinking someone would kidnap me because I'd wander off and talk to everyone in my path! I would knock on doors, introduce myself, explain my hobbies and ask if they had kids my age that would like to be my friend. You would often see Mom running down the street to bring me back home or finding me in the back yard with new friends from the neighborhood.

Mom brought my sister and I to Girl Guides. Although my sister loved Girl Guides, I didn't because, at the time, I was being teased by other girls about my naturally curly hair and I felt different. Mom enrolled us anyhow because she wanted us to enjoy an activity outside of school. I believe she felt it would help me with my confidence.

I hated Girl Guides at first. Sitting in the Team Leader's office one day with my arms crossed, all pouty-faced, I planned to tell her, "I don't want to go camping and get patches. I don't get along with the other girls."

However, as I looked around the office I saw a bunch of cases. Curious, I asked "What's in those boxes?"

She answered, "Those are Girl Guide Cookies."

"What do you do with them?"

"We sell them."

"How do you do that?"

"We give each girl a case and they go door to door or talk to their families. Things like that."

Well, my eyes bugged out. I asked for all the boxes that day but the Leader said "No."

Suddenly, I loved being a Girl Guide. All I wanted to do was sell cookies. Every day I'd go to the office and grab a case of cookies. I had my red wagon and my pretty dress. I looked like Shirley Temple. No one could say no to me.

I found my passion for sales that day. Mom still talks about it. "That's the day Tammy became a sales guru."

Selling comes natural to me. I love talking to people. Today I'm grateful for being introduced to Girl Guides but it wasn't for the usual things people think of, like camping and badges. Rather, Girl Guides taught me to find my natural passion and pursue it.

If you're an entrepreneur, find your own natural passion. A lot of people say they're passionate about something but they simply "borrow" passion from the stories of others. When you find the spark that sets your Soul on fire and you just can't sleep…well, that isn't just passion, it's your purpose. Pursue that and the Universe will open many doors for you!

Today, my business is in fashion and prestige skin care. I have an online fashion designer shopping mall. I've always been a girly-girl. Dressing up, jewelry, fashion bags, have always been a part of who I am, an extension of me on the outside. Combining that into a business platform that encompasses my daily lifestyle fits me perfectly.

I believe what we wear defines our personality. How we dress is how we show others who we are. Our fashion choices send others a message of what they can expect from us. We all do it. Even tribal communities identify themselves by the fashion choices they make.

The other thing you need to know about me is that I'm an Aquarius at heart, so I've always wanted to save the planet since I was a little girl. Asking me what I'd like to change in the world is a loaded question and we could probably start a reality TV show about it!

My answer may sound a little cheesy but I'd like people to feel gratitude and a part of something positive that's bigger than them. I listened to an amazing audio book, *The Four Agreements* by Don Miguel Ruiz and recommended to me by my dear friend and mentor, Ronen Triffon. This book opened my eyes to how we have been molded by society and taught how to think and behave.

The Four Agreements reveals the self-limiting beliefs that rob us of joy and create needless suffering. It offers a powerful code of conduct that can rapidly transform our lives to a new experience of freedom, true happiness, and love.

HARNESS THE POWER OF PASSION

I've not always had gratitude in my life. I've learned in the last two decades that it's not enough just to be grateful for the wonderful stuff. We must also to be grateful for the challenges we face.

I model that world change through my business and the personal growth it requires of me. I believe you must continuously move ahead and nurture an evolving state of mind. If you aren't, you just keep living the same year over and over. That's the definition of insanity—trying to overcome a challenge by repeating the same actions and expecting different results.

My first major business challenge occurred because of a partnership with a friend in 2015. That partnership ended distastefully. It literally felt like a divorce. I've been through one and this felt just like that. After it was over, I faced starting my business again from scratch with further hurdles ahead of me to overcome.

It took me a very long time to feel grateful for that experience. Finally, I realized I learned a lot about things I might have missed otherwise. It also taught me a lot about partnership rules and legalities and the questions I should have asked. Most importantly, I learned to not go into partnership with personal friends and especially without a contract from the beginning.

Those were tough lessons.

Another lesson I learned was about time and how we balance our lives. During one of my recent Coffee Talk Tuesday Episodes I spoke about how, as entrepreneurs, we put ourselves in non-stop work mode. If you're someone like me, you're passionate about what you do. That passion makes us feel we need to be "on" and in the game 24-7. We believe we must be on-line, responsive, posting daily, in attendance at every event, meeting, call…. It never shuts off.

At some point, we lose our sense of purpose and forget why we're doing this until finally, we burn out. We MUST take time off and we MUST get comfortable with saying the word "vacation" out loud and without apology.

I realize it can be difficult, especially when the people around us ask, "What do you mean, you're taking time off? Aren't you committed to your goal?"

Here's what I know for sure—we never reach our goals. We achieve milestones. Once we pass a milestone we reach for the next one. That's how entrepreneurs are wired. Often, we don't even take time to celebrate.

I like to use the analogy of sports because I'm a big hockey fan. Each game has three periods and in between periods, the players stop to take a break. They need that time to rejuvenate, to regroup and collaborate. They examine their performance and the game up to that point.

"Here's what we did really well...what worked...here's why our goalie didn't save that shot, or where defense needs to focus, etc."

They take a breather, review and then hit the second period. The break between the second and third periods is even longer because that last period is the most challenging. It's when every player is getting tired, but there is still a big fire in their bellies to win the game!

It should be the same way in our lives, our businesses and our projects. Reward yourself for accomplishments like completing a major event, closing a few great deals, beating your targets or achieving a new milestone.

No matter what you do for a living, you need a break between periods. That may be a full two-weeks or just 24 hours where you lock your phone away in a drawer so you can simply be present with yourself. It's taking time to evaluate, listen to your soul and reconnect.

HARNESS THE POWER OF PASSION

More importantly, enjoy quality time with the people in your life that may not be in business with you but have supported and loved you every step of the way. They, too, need time with you. These relationships are a major part of your life journey and should not be "sacrificed."

Here's the thing—not only do we need vacations; we also need to be okay with them. Have you ever taken time off but you're still answering email, still thinking about work? That's not "OFF."

Imagine shutting it off totally. What if you didn't post a tweet or check Facebook? Or if you did post, you shared a picture of your vacation and nothing else. Imagine being free from the guilt of taking the time you need and deserve. It's the only way to get back to 100% when you return to work mode. When you model balance between your personal life and business, you inspire others. It tells them that even when they are in total focused work-mode, it's okay to still enjoy what matters most.

Yes, there are times when you must go for the 30-day stretch, when you must go "get it done," but when it's over, make sure you reward yourself with down time. Every person is different in how long they need to press that refresh button but everyone needs to feel okay with it.

That's the change I'd like to see in North American businesses: people taking time for themselves, to listen to their inner voice and what the soul really wants. If you pay attention to European countries, they embrace that. It's part of their culture but here in North America, it's frowned upon. Imagine how much healthier, refreshed and inspired you would feel if you took a vacation?

Too often, people point a finger at Millennials, saying they're lazy and don't know what hard work is. I'm 43 and in my generation (and my mother's and grandmother's generations), it was 24-7 work-work-work. I believe the Millennials are smarter than that. We should be grateful to the Millennials and appreciate where they're trying to take us.

They are teaching us to value quality of life, not quantity of things. It's about embracing the day and truly being present for all those special moments we take for granted.

These experiences led me to where I am currently in my business. I've grown so much more observant to what's going on outside of me. I see and listen to key words people are saying. One of the terms I hear often is "E and E"—Exhausted and Excited. It's meant to inspire us.

In the past, I've used that phrase without thinking but I've since changed my perspective on it. Maybe it's because I'm in my 40s. (My grandmother did tell me wisdom would start kicking in around now.) These days, I pay attention to the words I use and the power of them.

When I was a young entrepreneur I listened to Tony Robbins, Jim Rohn, John Maxwell and others. I absorbed their words so I could change my mindset and improve my life choices. Recently, a switch happened. I've become the messenger to a following of people so I'm more watchful of the words I use. I pay attention and correct myself much more quickly. I feel my responsibility as a role model.

Tony Robbins and Les Brown still stand out for me as role models, not because of their motivational messages but because of their powerful life stories. Their experiences helped these men impact the world in a positive and uplifting way.

Tony's documentary "*I'm Not Your Guru*" showed me the man he truly is and what his purpose in life is. It opened my eyes to his troubling story of the mom who abused and belittled him while she desperately needed him in her life and was terrified to lose him. Surprisingly, that's what he is grateful for.

HARNESS THE POWER OF PASSION

He's grateful because those experiences drove him to learn about the psyche of the human mind, patterns, triggers and behaviors. It made Tony Robbins who he is today. His empire stemmed from the relationship with his mother.

Les Brown was fired from multiple radio stations and told he would never make it. Rather than quit, he emulated the successful people he wanted to be like. He adopted their style, their mannerisms and their words until he found his own style and message. He is the man he is today because he didn't quit and he found his true calling…his purpose. Today he teaches that each and everyone of us needs to expand and grow at every stage of our life and journey.

The other role model for me is Jim Carrey. Sure, he's an actor and one of my favorite comedians. It's easy to assume he's high energy and "on" all the time but I've noticed that his mindset and thoughts are very connected to the universe. He's a visionary and he taught me a lot about visualizing what I want in this life.

He even changed the way I do my vision board. I used to be that person who took a few pictures out of magazines, stuck them to poster board and said "Yup. There's my vision board."

However, those boards felt scattered and too general. I wasn't fully connected to it.

Jim Carrey's example taught me to visualize at a much deeper level. He talks about writing himself a cheque for a million dollars and visualizing himself receiving that cheque every single day until it happened. That opened my eyes to the power of seeing clearly what you want and knowing you deserve it. You just have to want it bad enough.

Someone taught me once (and I can't remember who), "Your 'Why' should be strong enough to make you cry." Then she took me through a process by asking me "What's your Why?"

I said, "My mom."

She answered, "Fine. What do you want for your mom?"

And I talked about this and that and she asked "Why?" again. And again.

She probably asked me "Why?" a hundred times, each time leading me to the next answer of what I wanted until we reached the deep emotion behind my Why.

Did it make me cry? Absolutely. It also helped me understand the true depth of my purpose.

Every single person I ask about their "Why," starts with material things. "To buy a fancy car. Pay off my mortgage. Travel the world. Renovate my house."

I know those surface answers are never enough to get them to do things they're afraid of, to overcome the fear we all have. They're not digging deep enough into their true Why.

You must take this exploration to the next level until you hit bedrock. As you go deeper and deeper by repeating the question "Why?" you start saying things that take on meaning until finally you reach the FEELING. That *feeling* overcomes your fears and excuses. Paying off a debt or taking a trip neve has that kind of power.

Then you must make it real.

For example, if you say you want a new house, describe what city it would be in? What type of community? Is it near a lake, or city central? What color is it? What size? Does it have a porch or a yard? What's in the yard? What do you smell in the air? Who is there with you? What do you hear?

Get really detailed and laser focused on your vision until it looks like a movie in your mind that you can play over and over again because you are crystal clear on it.

Today, the advice I'd give my younger self would be to forgive myself. Like I said, we all face challenges. I'd tell myself to have more gratitude, to be aware of my ego and be humble enough to listen to good advice. I'd also tell me to love myself by embracing the things I love and not allowing the opinions of others to hold me back.

I often feel the advice I give my daughter is like speaking to my younger self. Warning me about wolves in sheep clothes, embracing love, being kind, forgiving, tenacious, resourceful and adaptable, to develop a strong work ethic and always give the best of yourself.

Today, my business success provides me a platform and the credibility to be the change I want to see in the world. I host Coffee Talk Tuesday on FB Live where I teach people some of these lessons I've learned. I share the skills I gained from the challenges I've overcome. I show them how they can adapt, adjust their speech and mindset so they can succeed as well. I speak openly about what most people think of in their business or career but are afraid or intimidated to discuss. I also share practical business tools to help them with time management, scheduling and following up.

Most importantly, I share the gratitude I feel for all the challenges I've overcome and the people who guided me towards my purpose in life.

ABOUT TAMMY BOUCHER

Tammy resides in her Chic Suite in Edmonton, Alberta! She is blessed with a loving partner and an amazing 22-year-old daughter. She enjoys live entertainment/music, shopping, picnics, long walks and road trips to the great outdoors of Alberta.

She is also a wine connoisseur, constantly looking for the next great vino to enjoy along with a variety of restaurants and unique cultural dishes.

Over the last 20 years, Tammy has enjoyed careers as a Sales Development Coach, Recruiter & Manager. She has received numerous awards such as; Top Recruiter, Top Sales, Rookie of the Year, Most Valuable Leader, Rising Star & Leadership Award.

Highly involved with the United Way, she served as Chairperson for two years and was nominated for Chairperson of the Year for Small Business Award at their Red Tie Gala, 2017.

Tammy's strengths are in event planning, team training & personal coaching. She believes in inspiring others to grow past their fears and doubts and to have massive breakthroughs on their personal and business journey. She does this through her "Coffee Talk Tuesday FB Live," weekly episodes where she shares her experience both in business and career in a fun and relaxed environment.

She is grateful for the next generation of Millennials who are breaking the mold of old ways of thinking. She encourages their belief in working less while earning more, giving back to their communities and being grateful for every opportunity available to them.

Having a balanced life filled with a touch of chaos & challenge is what makes us stronger, more adaptable & resourceful.

HARNESS THE POWER OF PASSION

THE POWER OF YOUR WHY
by Benny Martin

From a young age, I knew for certain I wanted to be a mom. My dream was to nurture and raise my children to be happy and healthy as they grew up in a community filled with love and possibility.

In July 2015, I had my son and the world felt complete. However, what I didn't expect was a desire for more from life after the "baby bliss" passed.

My pregnancy was filled with uncertainty with unexpected health concerns for the baby. After my son was born we endured many specialist appointments, testing and a major surgery when he was just four months old that created a lot of anxiety and fear. The experience heightened my capacity to be grateful for all the good in my life but also made me eager not to waste my time and settle in life. It gave me strength and a desire to leave a legacy for my son.

As this was going on, I joined a motherhood circle for support, exploring the changes and challenges of becoming a mom. Through that community, I found a new perspective and the freedom to process what I really wanted to create for myself. I might not have been sure exactly what it was right then but I knew it would light me up again.

I realize now that prior to having my son and starting my business I was searching for something to challenge me. The longer I waited the harder it became to make any big change as I counted on the "security" of a salary, benefits and holiday time. It made me feel safe but at the same time, I was stuck.

After becoming a parent, one of the biggest lessons I learned was that the only thing I can count on in life is change (which has always been a challenge for me). When I finally accepted the challenge, and stepped out as an entrepreneur, there was no limit to how fast I grew. The harder I worked the more I was compensated and acknowledged for my effort. That was when I found real security.

I learned at a young age that for me to feel happy and alive I must continue to grow and expand. In my twenties that meant going to University, traveling the world and starting a career. Somewhere in my thirties I plateaued in my personal growth. It took me a long time to realize I was stuck. Making the decision to take the plunge into my own business was the hardest part for me. After that, it was simply figuring out how to make my dreams happen.

I knew nothing about being in business however I possessed many transferable skills from over ten years experience in the field of social services and solving problems so I moved ahead.

I also knew that any successful business starts with a passion you can get behind with all your heart. For me that passion has always been food combined with making a difference for people. I enjoy sharing my love of food with others. Growing up on a family farm and knowing where my food came from was important to me.

Combining my passion for good food with cooking classes along with my value of helping people eat well was the perfect fit for me. My goal is to leave them inspired to cook and eat healthy, delicious food. My business also became my platform for personal growth and gave me the opportunity to explore who I was and to prove to myself what I was capable of. I discovered an untapped drive to work harder and dig deeper than I ever had before. In the past, my life experiences often weighed me down but now I used them to drive me forward into the unknown.

Community has also been something I seek out in my life no matter where I go. I grew up in a small community where Sunday dinners and generosity to your neighbours was the norm. Today, it is a driving force in my business and raising my son. I choose to surround myself with like-minded people who share my value of creating positive social change.

Not long after launching my business, I attended a business rally that awoke in me a desire to take on a leadership role. Hearing the speakers, I realized I had something to share. I wanted to be the one on stage speaking, making an impact and inspiring others.

I was three months into my business and away from my son for the first time when I dug deep and found my personal "Why." It happened when I heard another business woman share her "Why" and it rattled me to the core. She said five words I will never forget.

"Your kids are watching you."

I felt a tickle in the back of my throat and my eyes welled up with tears. That was what I wanted—to raise my son to look up to his mom as someone who dreams big, hustles hard, gives with her whole heart and doesn't give up. It's my personal "Why" that makes me want to succeed and continues to pull me forward in a way I never experienced before.

The big life event of motherhood helped me tap into my powerful "Why."

Looking down at my baby that first time, I saw a blank slate of possibility. He wasn't born with self doubt, insecurities or excuses about why he couldn't do something. It made me aware how, as adults, we have so many reasons and excuses about why we can't. So many of us walk around, filled with self doubt. Our inner conversation sounds like "I don't matter" or "life isn't fair" which gets in our way of having and reaching our dreams and goals. It may be subtle or subconscious but as we grow up and experience pain and heartache we try to protect ourselves.

Being a role model for him and thriving in my business keeps me up at night with both excitement and determination. It also gives me the opportunity to *not* return to a full-time job which means I manage my own schedule. I have the freedom to be there for all the little and big moments of his life.

Less than one year after starting my business I separated from my partner which was another big life change to navigate, especially with an 18-month-old to care for. It took courage and strength to keep moving forward in a time of personal hardship and uncertainty. Getting up everyday, working my business and raising my son through the emotional turmoil was tough but that "Why" gave me fuel to keep going.

It took time to heal but I'm now happier and stronger as a mom and business woman.

Starting anything new always means a steep learning curve and becoming a mom and starting a new business at the same time took patience, resiliency and being gentle with myself. Today, whenever I work with a new entrepreneur the first thing I do is hand them an eraser. I share with them that my biggest lesson was not to be afraid to make mistakes or try something new. I give them permission from the beginning to mess up because that is how we learn.

I learned a lot about this by watching my son learn to walk. It was a three-month process that involved wobbling, a few steps forwards and falling down but he always got back up. Now he's running. I think about this every time I'm disappointed with a result or feel like a failure.

In business, you need to brush yourself off and get back up and not take yourself too seriously. If something doesn't work then learn from it and move forward. Seek coaching, take new actions but never beat yourself up. It's in those moments when you're about to give up but choose instead to push through when you create the biggest results and success.

The hard life experiences that rocked me became my biggest blessings. They'll be yours, too. In life, we can let uncertainty and doubt destroy us or, with time and support, we are empowered.

Building my business has been a lesson in being vulnerable and expanding my community. They say it takes a village to raise a child but I believe it also takes a village to grow a successful business. I learned to lean on others and ask for help, which also challenged me. Vulnerability is a hard thing to show but that authenticity strengthened my relationships with my friends, family, customers and team.

Knowing what drives me and having the support of an amazing community of mentors has been instrumental in my growth. I know whatever I do I will surround myself with people who challenge and inspire me to do more. Just a few months after starting my business I became a leader in the company I aligned with. I couldn't have moved with such velocity without the mentorship of others.

Sometimes I don't recognize myself. I've surprised myself with the results I've produced in such a short amount of time. As a leader, it's now my great privilege to pass on what

I've learned and mentor other women to succeed and reach their goals.

My motto this past year has been "Progress not Perfection" which helped me to keep taking small steps towards big goals. I have become stronger and braver than I ever knew was possible. My journey to motherhood and business involved challenge and hardship mixed with profound love and joy. Your business can also be the stage for you to stand on and prove to yourself what you're really made of.

I know my son is watching me. You have your own watchers. Be proud of what you accomplish and forgive yourself when you fall down. Life doesn't always go according to plan and in those moments, it's who we are that reveals our courage and abilities.

Align with your passions then go ahead and make mistakes. You'll be okay. You'll also create a story to inspire the community you create around you.

HARNESS THE POWER OF PASSION

ABOUT BENNY MARTIN

Benny Martin is passionate about sharing her love for healthy and delicious food through cooking classes as an Epicure Senior Leader and Consultant.

She is a hard-working single mom from Victoria, British Columbia, who previously worked in social services for over ten years, moonlighting as a food blogger to share her love of good food and recipes. After having her son, she experienced an AHA moment of wanting more out of life.

Her business was the perfect way to combine her love of food and desire to give back to my community through sharing clean eating and growing a team of like minded entrepreneurs. Best of all she found a way to stay home with her son, who is her world by sharing her passion for clean eating and continually stepping out of her comfort zone in her business.

With consistency and dedication in her first year of business she achieved over $50,000 in personal sales and over $100,000 in Organizational sales, she grew her team to include 25 consultants and promoted to Senior Leader, earning a trip to Portugal in February 2017.

She credits her business success to tapping into her "Why" and accepting coaching along the way. Benny loves mentoring other entrepreneurs to help them dream big and reach their goals.

A PASSION TO SERVE
by Pat Andersen

I hate writing. I'd rather stand in front of a large crowd and speak but when Candace asked me to contribute a chapter for this book, I agreed. It's all about taking personal responsibility which is a core value for me. I'm committed to sharing the story about my journey back to health and how everything I learned on that journey helped me create a successful business today.

My personal journey started back in 1967. The Viet Nam war was going on and my father was in charge of a military range. He was asked to test a spray to clear paths for tanks to train on, etc. It worked so darn good he thought "I'll bring some home."

So, Agent Orange came to the cottage. In turn, it wiped out a lot of my family.

I always say, "God's will" and look for the good in whatever happens. Because of my journey, I've helped a lot of Viet Nam vets and other people that have had chemical exposure but that's just been part of it. I get ahead of myself.

Because of my own challenges, I developed a passion for health. I accepted the responsibility of educating myself and completed a lot of courses in the holistic field to keep me alive. I've had my own ups and downs with my health but it's all been a piece of that journey.

I began my current business because the more I worked a traditional business model, the sicker I got. It wasn't where I needed to be. I didn't go back to school in the holistic field to have an office. I'm not a 9-5'er.

Today, I'm aligned with a network marketing company that offers products to improve our well-being and a compensation income that rewards hard work. I teach others that, unless we take responsibility for our own health, we're not going to get better. In fact, we're going to get worse. I have the experience and the tools to show people how they can change that cycle.

It's actually been a lot of fun. I am now the Top Female Distributor of the company I'm with because I have a passion for the products. I've seen the difference they make. I also love to see people take responsibility for their lives so I guess you could say my real passion is teaching people how to take control over both their health and wealth. I built a successful business because of my passions.

That's why I feel I can honestly say to be successful in any business and to create change; you must be passionate about what you do.

Today, when someone tells me they need to change, the very first thing I say to them is "Are you coachable? If you're not coachable, if you're not willing to make the changes, I can't help you. It's just not going to happen."

If they answer "Yes, I'm ready," then I'm willing. "Come on!"

I'm a stickler but I have an 80-20 rule when I change people's eating habits. We're going to cheat. We're not going to be perfect but if we don't allow ourselves to cheat a little we're not going to stick with anything. But how BAD that 20 is... well, that's another conversation.

The first thing we do is review the things they currently eat. I ask them to give me a week's food journal and warn them not to lie and not to leave anything out. I don't care if it's only ten Reese's Pieces. I can't help until I know the truth.

After that first week, we look at their journal together and I ask, "Do you think you could cut ONE of those ten out today? And tomorrow, cut it down to 8?" I make it so simple they don't even realize they're making better choices.

We take it one step at a time and make it as easy as possible. I have a Facebook page called Naturally Lean and Healthy. I post recipes and motivational stuff. I like it to be fun while I get them outside their normal box.

When I moved to the area I now live in, I was asked to do meetings and talks, stuff like that. I came across a family that weighed maybe 900 pounds between the three of them. They sat in one of my meetings with their arms crossed and just glared at me the whole evening.

At the end of the meeting they were very rude and remarked, "We got told we needed to come here because of our son."

I'm looking at this boy thinking he's 13-14 years of age and yes, he was overweight. Then I found out he was just 6-years-old.

I looked at them and because I'm a truth teller, said "What you're doing is committing the worst child abuse I've ever seen."

I then turned to the boy and asked, "Do you have any friends?"

He started crying and answered, "No. They make fun of me and call me the Fat Little Boy."

I noticed he wore cowboy boots so I asked, "Well, can you ride your horse?"

He shook his head. "I can't get on my horse anymore."

"Do you play any sports?"

"No, they won't pick me for a team."

By now the parents were crying so I turned to them and said, "You need to change. You can't change him until you change you."

I spent a lot of time helping that family, especially the young boy. He was cute because he'd call me up and tell me, "Mom cheated...Dad did this...." It got to the point where they didn't do anything because they knew they would get tattled on. It became kind of funny.

Today, that young boy won the state wrestling championship three years in a row.

Do they still struggle? Of course, they do. We all have a lifetime of habits to overcome.

That's what we can do, one family at a time in any place but people need to care enough to want to make a difference. Whatever your business product or service, you need to care, one family, one person at a time.

I've always been a change kind of person. Either we want it or we don't. We can either sit and wallow in self-pity or we can make the changes. It's one or the other. There is no in-between.

So how does this help you use your business to create positive change?

First, take care of your health. Without it, nothing else is important.

Second, don't waste time. Find the people who are willing to make a change, who declare themselves coachable. If someone doesn't want to help themselves, simply walk away because there's nothing you can do. Not everyone wants to get better or improve their lives. They're quite happy having other people feel sorry for them. Personally, I don't understand this but I've learned to use the word "NEXT" around people like this.

Be a product of your own product or service whether you own a traditional business or are a network marketing professional. Because of my own journey, I learned how vital it is to take care of myself first. That means I come from a place where *I know* the difference I can make. Confidence and passion attracts and engages.

Then, make sure what you are voicing is worth hearing. I always tell my team to "Speak to the Listening." Unless you have information pertinent to your client or customer, no one will bother to listen to you. Remember, it's all about the Listener, not You.

Build a solid, successful business through training, customer service, and servitude by always putting their needs before your own. However, I also believe in balance. Everyday I do something for me...whether it is golfing, reading or playing with my horses. Find your balance.

Believe in your dreams. Work hard to achieve what you were meant to do and to be. Never allow anyone to take those dreams away from you.

I want to be remembered for my caring and for changing people's health. I truly want people to be successful in their lives and I will work hand in hand to help them with their goals and dreams. That's why, even though I hate to write, I was willing to contribute this chapter.

HARNESS THE POWER OF PASSION

ABOUT PAT ANDERSEN

Pat Andersen lives in Oklahoma on her horse training and breeding facility with her husband. She received the National Association of Professional Women's "Woman of the Year Award 2012/2013" in the Health and Wellness Profession. Her passion is for empowering women to be the best version of themselves.

STEP FOUR

Find

YOUR MENTORS

Many receive advice, only the wise profit from it.
~ Harper Lee ~

LETTERS FROM DAD
by Heather Andrews

In a split second, my life changed.

It was 5:00 a.m. in Saudi Arabia when the phone rang. The noise woke up my roommate.

"It's your mom," she said, handing me the phone.

My gut tightened. Dread. What time was it back home?

"Hello?" I strained to understand my mom. She was crying.

"There's has been an accident," she said. Questions raced through my mind. "And, your dad… Well, is gone."

In physical agony, I crumbled to the floor and the tears came in a torrent. I didn't know if they would stop.

Her phone call 20 years ago still echoes like it was yesterday. On March 10, 1997, my mom became a widow. My siblings and I became fatherless.

Dad was 62. I was 26 and pregnant with a child my dad would never meet. All I could think was, "Why?" He was my dad and I needed him.

Why?

My first clear thought was that I needed to go home to Canada immediately and be with my family. My roommate was a gift from God on that day. She called my fiancé and then sat with me, held me and reminded me, just by her presence, that I wasn't alone.

I had never known such pain. I was living a nightmare. I wanted to go back to sleep and wake up to go to work like any other day.

Why?

In difficult times, when your own strength fails, the strength of others carries you through. My inner circle of friends packed up my apartment and moved everything to my fiancé's Saudi Arabian residence.

To this day, I am grateful to my friends and my employer who had one focus: to get me home to my family. It struck me later that some of the most important lessons my dad instilled in me would be proven in the hours and months that followed his death.

He would have told me: *Surround yourself with good, solid, true people.*

As I prepared to leave Saudi Arabia, with the help of my fiancé, friends and colleagues, I knew I had done that.

Within 24 hours of my mom's phone call, I was on a plane headed halfway around the world. On the 12-hour flight, my thoughts were spinning. I wondered desperately how my mom would go on alone.

Another lesson from Dad: *Take care of your family.*

I would help her. Mom had already been on stress leave caring for him after a farming accident three months prior left him without the use of one arm.

I thought how grateful I was to have seen him at Christmas. He was eagerly anticipating his grandchild. I tried to remember what I said to him as I hugged him at the airport after that visit. My pain lessened just a little when I remembered: "I love you Dad. Thank you for all you have done for me."

Hug the ones you love, he always said.

When I arrived home in Calgary, Alberta, my mom and I held each other for a long time. I had never hugged her so tight. Even at that low moment, she shared her strength, thinking she had to be there for her kid. There is nothing like a mother's love.

When we separated, all I could say was, "Why?"

"I don't know," she said. "But it was his time."

In our family home, the only home I'd ever known, things didn't feel quite right. In my parents' bedroom, his shirt hung over the back of a chair ready for him to put it on. The top of his dresser was cluttered with his things. His pajamas were folded up under his pillow, ready and waiting for a sleep that had already begun.

It didn't make sense that he wasn't coming back.

I listened to the answering machine message just to hear his voice.

There was a note on the kitchen counter from Dad. It was for my mom, written before Dad left the house 48 hours ago. "Gone to bank, be back soon. Love you!"

Time froze for me. Everything moved slowly as I absorbed the empty feeling of a house filled only by memories. At just 26 years of age, had I been taking life for granted? The fragility of life became so clear.

In the days before the funeral, our friends, family and neighbors brought food and cleared snow from our rural property. The kindness that came our way made us feel special beyond words.

Another Dad lesson sunk in: *Love and respect always.*

Five days after the phone call, a limousine took us to the funeral home. Mom had not slept in days. I worried how she and my siblings would make it through the day.

The service was a wonderful celebration of his life. Mom chose the song "How Great Thou Art," a song from their wedding day 39 years earlier. The singer's voice was magic. As the words poured out and the organ rang, it was the most beautiful I had ever heard it sung. I still hear it.

As we drove to the burial site, I felt detached, like I was watching a sad movie. I wanted someone to wake me up from the nightmare. Numbed, I don't know who stood beside me and hugged me as we said goodbye and laid flowers on his casket.

At the reception, the sheer volume of people waiting for us struck me. More than 500, I learned later. A well-known entrepreneur in our community, my dad connected with everyone. As person after person shared a cherished story about my dad, the nightmare faded just a bit. I started to think it might be possible to heal, someday. We shared laughter and celebrated a life taken too soon.

Knowing my dad touched each of these people in his own way during his lifetime comforted me. Dad always encouraged us to *be true to ourselves*. He lived that way, always being present and connecting honestly with the people who entered his life. A man of integrity, honor and respect, he loved his family to bits and was loved back so fully.

Over the next few days, family left and Mom and I began to live our lives one day at a time. The two of us had an acreage with lots of work to do and I had a baby to grow. However, as the months passed, Mom came to the difficult decision to move to town; the acreage was too much work alone.

It was a full-time job downsizing to prepare the acreage for sale. Like most farming homes, there was a huge barn, outbuildings and a shop where Dad fixed farm equipment and vehicles. The amount of stuff seemed overwhelming. Where do you even begin while still wracked with grief?

Mom and I threw ourselves into the hard work. I tried to think what Dad would have said if he were there with us. *Work hard and be grateful.* I remembered him fixing his equipment, singing along to the radio in his garage that was set up just the way he liked it.

We kept some sentimental items, sold others at auction and gave some away. I felt nausea in the pit of my stomach with each item that left. One less piece of my dad I could hold. I cried while I worked.

In June, the home where I'd lived for 22 years was sold. Mom bought a lovely home in town soon after to begin the next chapter of her life. She was so strong. She's still the strongest person I know.

My fiancé arrived home six months after we'd last seen each other. I was overheated and very pregnant, but so excited to see him. Living my own love story, I watched him come through the airport gate. I smiled and my heart sang for the first time in months. All I wanted to do was hold him for days. I would have run into his arms, but I could only waddle.

We were ready to welcome our baby into the world, but first we had to take care of one detail: the wedding.

That week, we held a small ceremony in my parents' front yard surrounded by family, friends and an incredible amount of love, the likes of which I haven't felt since. It was the last major event held at the home my parents raised their family in. I felt Dad with us and he knew that I was happy, my mom was safe and we were moving forward.

A few days later, as my husband and I explored Banff in the stunning Canadian Rocky Mountains, our child decided to make a debut.

When I went into labor, I felt petrified, excited and sad all at once. Petrified, as I wasn't sure what to expect. Excited that our baby was finally joining us. Sad that my dad would never hold his grandchild.

Weighing in at six pounds, 14 ounces and 19 inches long, our wonderful little baby boy arrived. He looked so much like his grandpa's side of the family.

My dad had mentioned on my Christmas visit that if his grandchild was a girl, Shania would sure be a great name. (Subtle, Dad.) In honor of my dad, the ways he touched this world, the lessons he taught, and his unconditional love, we named our son Shane.

If ever I felt like angels moved among us, it was the moment I held Shane for the first time. I finally understood how much my dad loved each of his kids. I understood why he cried every time I got on the plane back to Saudi Arabia.

I said a prayer that day, asking Dad to always watch over Shane and keep him safe.

My new husband and I returned to Saudi Arabia for another two years before settling back in Canada to raise our family. Our three children are now teenagers and I've passed my dad's lessons onto them. He would have been so proud of them. My mom remarried and today is an incredible grand-mother and our kids love her to bits.

Tell your loved ones how special they are to you, Dad would have said.

Now, I have my own lesson to add.

Live a life full of experiences. Love hard, love lots. Live for the present.

Use your business in the same way. Love hard. Love lots.

ABOUT HEATHER ANDREWS

Heather is a lifestyle strategist who works with women who want to live the stellar life they deserve. She helps them say YES to a better life by saying NO to the obstacles in their path.

When her husband was deployed to Afghanistan, she created a secret formula to raising children as a solo parent. Today, Heather has a career, an online business, and is raising three teenagers.

With her experience and certifications as a healthcare professional, manager, change mentor, and health coach, she is the founder of *Follow It Thru Health Coaching* and creator of the *Mom on the Go* program.

Eager to help others share their stories of inspirational change, Heather is publishing a forthcoming compilation book, coming December 2017.

THE ABC PATH
by Michelle Wright

In twenty years, I will be 74. What I'm doing at that age or where I will be, is determined by what I choose today, and every day between now and 74. I envision myself as a sassy and smart 74-year-old, dancing, riding horses and challenging my boundaries every day. So where to start, to be that amazing 74-year-old? (or 84, 94 or 104!).

First, I need to listen to my current and future self and honor my past self. My current voice can be extremely intuitive, my future voice is inspirational and aspirational, and my past voice is full of recognition and acknowledgement.

So, when I'm faced with a choice to get up or sleep in, connect or close off, self-care or self-indulge, I ask what would the 74-year-old me do, compared to what I'm choosing today?

I'm pretty sure she'd get up, get connected and look after herself! That future sassy self is a butt kicker. Who am I to complain about doing something to further my dream when that old girl is saying "Do it now. Do the best you can, and create a life with no regrets."

I'm aware that this hesitation to act on my dream is habit. It keeps me safe, lets me avoid fear, and makes me believe I'm the most aware person on the planet. I listen so well to myself, honestly, I should be a yogi! In reality, I'm scared or bored or procrastinating and I use the awareness card to stay where I am.

"That's a bit scary, so let's just think about it for a while and find a million other things to do to avoid feeling..."

I am good at just...waiting...it...out. The idea passes and I stay in my comfy cocoon, feeling fearless but avoiding fear and convincing myself I'm incredibly self-aware.

The truth is I'm just a good hesitator.

However, fear is a valid emotion to listen to. Just as valid as joy, or excitement or anticipation except it has a bad rap. "Push past the fear," "Be courageous," "Fear is for sissies" shout the Pinterest quotes, but as a life coach, I know ignoring a feeling, any feeling, stands in the way of my best life. I need to be in the feeling, and FEEL it, to pull myself through it and into new possibilities. Exploring fear (or any feeling) and pausing to reflect on where that feeling comes from, tells me so much more about what to do than if I ignore it and try to power through.

What is my fear mostly about?

Lack of preparation is usually the culprit. When I'm not ready to give the speech or when I neglect my riding confidence, or if I'm daydreaming and another driver cuts me off—I'm simply not ready and fear literally takes the reins.

When I'm prepared, I am rarely afraid.

However, over-preparation is at the perfection end of the scale and I find myself stuck again. I can't post a Facebook ad because it's not perfect! I can't go to a networking event because I don't have a chill-inducing elevator pitch! I'm not at the perfect weight! My roots are showing! On and on, a million and one PERFECT excuses!

The solution for when fear and the pursuit of perfection prevents me from getting things done? My 74-year-old self of course!

FIND YOUR MENTORS

She blows off perfection without any trouble, and lets me know in no uncertain terms that "No one really cares about your perfect performance. They're probably worrying about what everyone thinks of them!"

Ballsy broad eh?

Now, I don't mean that everyone runs around being callous and isolationist, only thinking of themselves. Many people do great things and make other's lives amazing. They do it, not because they want people to think well of them but because it makes *them* feel good! We're talking real positive change and amazing contributions to the world. They're not waiting until they get perfect before they get out there and make a difference!

I'm thankful for those people. They inspire me to act when I feel afraid or get caught up in perfectionism.

My sister was one of that group. She always seemed to be doing the right thing for herself while still caring about others. She didn't worry about what they thought about her. Hundreds attended her funeral and spoke of the strong connection they felt with her. She lived life her way, unfettered by the need for others' approval.

To honor what Big Sis instilled in me, I have a reminder I use to keep me moving along my own path:

A – Approve of myself

B – Take care of Business

C – Connect

D – Divinity

E – Energize

Whenever I feel stuck and can't get motivated, I run down my list to see if I've been sliding on one or another. Often, I am. When my spices are alphabetized or the house looks like a magazine cover and the business doesn't seem to be gaining traction, I know I've been avoiding some part of that ABCDE reminder.

A = Approve of myself is where the start and it's my biggest challenge.

My sister approved of me. Always. She was proud of me during my divorces, when I was wasting my talents in poor career choices and astonishingly even when I was enjoying a really good pity party.

So, when I use perfection as an excuse to procrastinate, I hear her voice (and my 74-year-old self) saying *"You're amazing, achieving great things. You have a life others aspire to have. You're just perfect exactly the way you are."*

I mean seriously, how reasonable is it to think I can't give an inspiring speech to a group or absolute attention to a client because I haven't lost 30 pounds? Do I really believe my creativity dries up because my roots are showing? I'm pretty sure no scientific research supports either of those two "perfection" theories.

That's why I choose to approve of myself, regardless of any perceived standards I may meet or miss.

Armed with all that self-confidence, I should knock the world's socks off, right? That takes me to B = Take care of Business.

Whether it's my corporate role, my rancher role, or my entrepreneurial role, I must do the work or I feel crappy and won't get the results that 74-year-old me or Big Sis know I can deliver.

Oh, sure, manifesting desires and setting intentions is powerful stuff but only if I get out of bed to meet the Universe at the door!

For me, I find putting myself out there through marketing and networking difficult but it must be done if I want to change the world with my contribution. In order to help my clients create their best lives, it makes sense they must know about me before they can benefit from our interaction!

This is where fear can easily sidetrack me so how do I get motivated enough to take care of the business of marketing?

That's through C = Connect.

I love connecting with others so what could be easier than looking at the dreaded marketing work as a way to connect instead of a way to sell? By changing my focus, I eliminate the fear.

Some basic coaching skills are brilliant for creating connection. If you're struggling to make connections I suggest taking at least one session of coach training because coaching is all about connection. It teaches you how to meet the other person in the moment and place they are at and ask powerful, curious questions. When you realize you don't have to fix people, you'll be hooked like I was.

Through these resonating conversations, we can discover great possibilities and joy. Sounds heavenly, right?

Which brings us to D = Divinity.

I believe divine grace supports me constantly. This grace approves of me, helps me take care of business, and connects me to myself and to others. It is a vibration as much as a belief that hums throughout the day (as long as I'm listening) joining us all together.

When the external noise level gets too high, and my fear or perfectionism seems to be rising, pausing for a moment to meditate or open a space for the divine is powerful. (Wow, just writing those words brings a serenity to the space I'm in.)

Do you feel the energy associated with each of the words we've explored so far? I find A and D calm, and B and C more invigorating. What about you?

Which brings us to the last reminder, E = Energize.

Energize is the "Shake it, move it, get the blood pumping now!" reminder! It's what creates that dancing 74-year-old I want to be because I'm dancing now. In the car, the office, my workshop, I'm grooving! I'm moving! And when my butt is numb from sitting at the desk, or my back is kinked from sanding furniture for three hours, I get out for a vigorous walk.

Movement energy makes me joyful!

There is also the energy of choice and being multi-passionate about many things.

When I'm told by the business gurus "Do only one thing," "Focus," "Stay true to your brand" I get dizzy! When the gurus demand "Name your passion" I respond with more than one: coaching, farm cleanups and heirloom rescue.

I know my passions. I'm following my heart. I see no reason to limit myself. If a new passion comes along, I will embrace it! Just like the reminder phrase is only five out of 26 letters of the alphabet: A—Approve of myself, B—Take care of Business, C—Connect, D—Divinity and E—Energize, there are many more passions I plan to discover and pursue!

By taking fear and perfectionism out of the equation I wish for you a life of limitless passions and possibilities, the energy to sustain all of them and the joy that comes with making a difference, your way.

Namaste!

ABOUT MICHELLE WRIGHT

"I've been on the planet over 50 years, and I'm still searching and seeking out all the cool things I can do, might do, will do!"

Michelle Wright's journey has included creating a unique service to farmers, helping them with their spaces. This was born out of a corporate role, where she spent many years working with rural landowners and felt "the call" to do more for these amazing folks.

Michelle knows she's no guru but rather a guide, helping folks to develop their "best self and best life," whether it's space and stuff related, or just plain life. She cherishes the opportunities to work with her coaching, farm cleanup or heirloom rescue clients. Every day provides something new and interesting.

She hopes you enjoy the chapter as she had fun writing, editing and reviewing it with Candace and her cohorts. Sharing is what adventures are all about!

Michelle lives on a quarter horse ranch near Smoky Lake, Alberta, with 15 horses, 4 dogs, and her husband Dennis. She is a step-mom of 3, and grannie of 8.

STEP FIVE

FALL DOWN &
Recover

*I didn't get there by wishing for it or
hoping for it, but by working for it.*
~ Estée Lauder ~

NEVER SETTLE
by Tammy Kirton

It is said we all have a defining moment, a moment usually stemming from an experience in our childhood. It's a moment that shaped us into who we are today. The defining moments of my life led me to know when to put myself first and become courageous and determined.

My name is Tammy Jean Kirton. I'm 42 years old. This is my story.

It was supposed to be a fun day going to the movies with my father and brother. Little did I know my whole world was about to change.

My father was leaving. He and my mom were getting a divorce. Then he asked the million-dollar question, "Who do you want to live with?"

At 5 years old, well, you can just imagine.

I wanted to choose my dad but instead chose my mom because I didn't want to hurt her feelings. That one decision led me to a life where I worried about what others thought of me, made decisions based on everyone else's opinions and worried about how they would feel.

My brother and I lived with our mom until the day came when she had a nervous breakdown. Now we had no choice but to go live with our father and his girlfriend except my father was never there. His job took him out of town for the week and even weeks on end.

I grew up being an emotional eater—not that I understood it then. People close to me teased me, called me a FAT COW and GOODYEAR BLIMP. When you hear those words over and over at a young age from the very ones supposed to love you, you believe it to be true. Soon it didn't matter what I looked like because all I saw in the mirror was someone who was fat.

Basically, I grew up never loving myself, having no self respect and not feeling worthy. Deep inside I lacked confidence in myself. I had no idea how to love or be loved, always thinking. "If I just lost weight I would be lovable."

In my teenage years, I looked for the love and attention I never got from my father from boys and experimented with drugs. All things that led down a very dark road.

In my early twenties, I met a man who became my husband and father of my 3 beautiful children. He showed me a life I never dreamed of but in a material way. This was his way of showing his love.

From the outside looking in, everything seemed great. I had a nice place to live and a wonderful career as an esthetician. I basically had a life built for me but deep inside, I was lonely and I blamed my husband for not making me happy.

I traded the things I valued or considered foundational pillars in a relationship—communication, honesty and trust. I told myself, "It's ok if you don't have communication because you have material things."

However, I wasn't true to myself and that became my biggest obstacle. It kept me in a relationship that should have ended a lot sooner than it did.

I allowed myself to get emotionally beat below the ground. My self talk was extremely negative. I left the relationship because HE didn't make me happy only to return a short time later because we were going to work on things. This began a vicious circle repeated over the next 20 years.

I share this experience because I always told myself I wouldn't be one of those women who stayed in a relationship because they didn't think they deserved more or because of the kids, or they felt they were too old to leave.

After *almost* leaving for the 3rd time, I asked myself, "Why wasn't I happy?"

At that moment, I realized I wasn't unhappy with myself. I didn't feel loved the way I thought I should because I didn't love myself.

My journey of change began soon after. I took a hard look at myself and in 2003, along with a good friend, took a personal development course called Landmark Forum. The program showed me my defining moment and how it had shaped me.

Shortly after, I discovered the world of Direct Sales, which I see as personal development at it's finest. The profession allowed me to dream again. It showed me there is so much more to life and anything is possible. I experienced a few different opportunities but one thought stuck with me that has served me well.

"You've got to be passionate about what you do."

Fast forward to Dec 2014. Having reached an all-time high of 220 lbs and then losing a bit of that, I finally made the decision to put myself first. It was finally time to take care of me—physically and emotionally.

Since my late teens, I dreamt of getting stage to compete in a bodybuilding competition. After growing up in an environment of loneliness and shame and the struggles it produced, a competition like this would be my ultimate achievement. It represented commitment, determination, perseverance. I had stopped and started so many times in the past and achieving this goal would signify true strength.

Quite frankly, I was sick and tired of being sick and tired.

My journey to the stage began, with my eye on May 2015 for my first show. However, I hit a plateau I couldn't get past for three months. After talking it over with my trainer, I pushed my show date to October 2015.

I didn't give up my goal, only adjusted the timeline because I didn't want to hate the journey.

The most valuable piece of advice my trainer gave me was to acknowledge my success along the way. He also advised me to think about who I was becoming and who I would be after leaving the stage.

He helped me visualize the stage and that moment of stepping onto it. It became so real for me that I physically felt the excitement. I could close my eyes any time and feel that energy and it made me want to just go.

I laser-focused on that stage. Finally, the day came. For the first time in my life, I had accomplished an important personal goal. However, I still had some challenges to face.

While it was an amazing experience, I found myself wishing my dad had been there. Deep down I still wanted his acknowledgment. Even though he said he was proud of me, the little girl trying to prove herself still existed.

Unfortunately, around this same time, life also kept happening. Right before the competition my mother had a medical emergency and it fell on me to take her to the hospital. Just after the competition, I left my husband once again, took my children and went back to work full time.

But what honestly set me back was seeing my stage photos. My first thought was, "OMG did I seriously look like that?"

I felt disgusted with my pictures. The image in my head and the photos didn't match up. I wasn't lean enough...still had cellulite...all my stretch marks showed... The list went on and on.

All the things that over time would change. (Well except those stretch marks.) My trainer said it best. "Those pictures will be the worst of your best."

I took my eyes off what was important, acknowledging my daily, weekly and monthly successes. Instead of looking at how far I had come, I focused on where I wasn't. I compared myself to the girl that won. I allowed all these circumstances to pull me down and I fell back into old habits.

Not putting myself first caused me to gain back 40 pounds before I course corrected.

One of my biggest breakthroughs happened when I *consciously* decided to eat something not on my plan. Being an emotional eater most of my life, this was huge for me. Making a mindful choice allowed me to fully enjoy what I was eating without guilt. Before that moment, I ate because I was happy, sad, angry...you name it. No more.

Today, I understand what it means to struggle, to not feel good enough and like a failure because of all my previous attempts at losing weight. My vision is to help at least one person not give up. I was always great at starting new plans but they only lasted 1-2 weeks max. Not any more.

Joining forces with a nutritional cleansing company allowed me to release 20 of the 40 pounds I gained without depriving myself. Not having the physical time to eat and prep my meals like I used to, the flexibility and simplicity of the system gave me back control. There is no magic pill. From my experience, it comes down to the right balance of nutrition and physical exercise.

FALL DOWN AND RECOVER

I'm excited about stepping on the stage again. It might not even be a body building event. It might be speaking to other women. I just know there's a stage in my future.

Here is what my experience taught me.

We all have triggers…triggers that can derail us, if we allow them to. In the beginning, I got derailed a lot, but each time I started again and looked back to learn what those triggers were. This gave me valuable insights into the role my thoughts played, how I reacted to situations and what to do in the future to prepare myself for the next time.

I also learned that, yes, there will be a next time. It may not look the same but life always challenges us, for this is how we grow. I look back now and know I was meant to go through everything to be where I am today.

I missed out on opportunities three times in my esthetics career to be an educator because of self sabotage. In fact, I almost did it again with this opportunity. To be part of this collaboration of other amazing ladies is very humbling and affirming.

Being an esthetician for 20 years was rewarding but after going through my weight loss experience, my focus shifted. My passion now is to help other people feel good about themselves. We only have one body to live in and we deserve it to be the best it can be.

I am not a quitter and I want to show my children they can achieve anything in this life, too. At some point in your own life you will be faced with the choice to go after your dreams and goals. You must believe you are worth it. Whatever you may have experienced in your past, the power to achieve lies within you. Changing your self talk is the beginning.

Loving yourself is not selfish. It is a requirement. How can you be loved or love someone else if you don't love yourself first? It took me a long time to accept that truth and I'm still on the path.

You will be faced with what may seem insurmountable challenges or obstacles. With every fall you have, get back up. You will learn something each time about the strength and courage to push on. Every day take steps and make decisions that push you further on your journey.

Never allow yourself to fall into the habit of comparing your path to someone else's. Rather, practice looking behind at the progress you've made. No matter how slow it may seem, every step forward is still in the right direction.

Every one of you has a story to tell. We never know how it may impact another person. I encourage you to tell yours.

FALL DOWN AND RECOVER

ABOUT TAMMY KIRTON

For twenty years, Tammy Kirton has been an esthetician and award-winning nail technician. Competing in her first Figure competition has allowed her to pursue a new passion while her love for helping people feel good has evolved since her stage debut in 2015.

She lives in *not-sure-what-the-weather-will-be* Alberta, Canada with her beautiful teen daughter and 2 energetic boys. She plans to keep on inspiring them to never give up and become the best they can be.

When she's not preparing for her next competition or helping a client or playing taxi mom to her busy kids, you will find her enjoying walks around the nearby lake, spending time with friends, getting zen with yoga or enjoying a glass of wine with the ladies.

BEGIN AGAIN
by Clara Ball

I am excited to share my story with you and honored to be in the company of these amazing women. If someone told me a year ago I'd be writing to encourage women entrepreneurs or I'd win the 2017 Womanition Award for Philanthropy, I'd have laughed out loud.

If you're starting your own business or simply thinking about starting one, I applaud you. It's not an easy choice. I also know a commitment to yourself and your own success can be the easiest promise to break. You may even be thinking, "OMG, what am I doing, this is crazy!" but don't worry, that's perfectly normal.

That's why I agreed to share my journey.

Frankly, I don't consider myself the best example. I had no choice except to start my own business because I couldn't find a job. I needed to create my own. I did everything backwards. In fact, I had so many things happening at the same time, I worried my brain might explode. Even now, I'm not as organized as I could be. I don't have a completed business plan (working on that now). Frankly, it's embarrassing and here's the kicker... I had no money to start.

But hey, you know what? I didn't let those conditions stop me from making it happen. My belief, vision and purpose are undeniable. I'm confident the Law of Attraction is on my side because everything keeps working out for me.

Three years ago, however, I didn't believe that. In fact, the opposite was true because I found myself living with friends I had simply come to visit. Everything I'd worked for in the previous eight and a half years suddenly disappeared. I was broke, without a car and no job.

In 2006, I left my job of ten years as a graphic designer for Yellow Pages to travel for a year with my 18-year-old daughter. We went first to Egypt and then to the United Arab Emirates. However, after a couple of weeks in the UAE, my daughter decided she wasn't ready for this trip and wanted to come home. I respected her wishes and sent her ahead while I stayed on.

When we said good-bye, we thought it was a temporary separation. I had no idea my one year journey would turn into an eight and a half year stay. I fell in love with the UAE and got a contract at a Ladies College, teaching a course in Secretarial Skills to a group of local women who worked for an oil company. I didn't let the fact I had never been a secretary or teacher stop me.

"After all," I thought, "How hard could it be, creating and delivering a course for ladies who hardly spoke English in a field I had never worked in or learned about?"

Surprisingly, not only was the course a great success, it became highly recognized by the UAE government as the first of its kind for Emiratization (a government initiative to get local women into the workforce). For me this was a big win. It provided me the confidence I needed to move forward in life believing I could do anything I set my mind to.

Belief in yourself and what you are doing is paramount for success.

I went on from there to positions in administration management and executive personal assistant roles for a few years, but I knew I was meant for something with more meaning and purpose. I just hadn't figured out what it was.

When the economy fell apart and jobs disappeared, finding work became a challenge. Once again, hard decisions were demanded from me. I required work, needed a visa and wanted to do something that helped others.

I knew there was a strong need for effective communication skills in a country populated with more expats than locals. I loved teaching and strongly believed helping women develop skills in a male-dominated society would be beneficial.

I found three other people also looking for an opportunity to work independently. We formed FAB Solutions (Freelance and Business Solutions) and launched a Freezone business in Dubai. This would allow us to work in our respective fields, obtain the required resident visas and split the costs involved.

Looking back, this was not my best idea. Because I was the founder and general manager, all the responsibility fell on me. When things went south with my partners, I was unprepared and in financial distress.

About that time, I returned to Canada for a friend's wedding. While there, I learned the Freezone company considered my trip as absconding and avoiding my responsibility. As you can imagine, it was not a good position to be in.

Faced with the heart-wrenching choice to stay in Canada or risk legal action in Dubai, I stayed in Canada to rectify a situation I couldn't resolve over there. The whole experience has been humiliating, humbling and a big wake-up call about being accountable for my choices and actions.

*Make sure you know exactly where you stand
in any business venture and every possible
outcome should something go wrong.*

Ultimately, this wedding guest turned into a full-time roommate for my friends and created a year of devastation and heartache for me. It was like being plucked out of my life over there to uncertainty here.

So, at a not-so-young age, I started over. Again.

The next couple of years put me on the entrepreneurial roller coaster just trying to make ends meet. I held a variety of freelance jobs, coming up with one idea or another. I cannot even begin to share how many little brochures I created trying to market myself.

All this effort came from a place of desperation created from an environment where I was bombarded with bill collector pressure. (Yet another reason I am going on a gypsy journey, complete with caravan).

I can tell you from experience, desperation is a terrible emotion to start a business on. I felt pressure from everyone to do this...try that...apply for this job...you have skills...you should just get a job and every other judgment you can imagine about why I wasn't successful.

I can tell you, none of it helped. Rather it just replaced belief with doubt. Everyone has an opinion, which they are entitled to but it's their point of view. Listen to objective advice but the only one you really must believe in is you.

Trust your instincts. Your emotions are your guidance system. If it doesn't feel good, don't do it.

I have never been shy and love meeting people everywhere I go. At a local market in Dubai, I met one woman who led me to the path I am now on.

Beth Lamont is a beautiful soul who moved my heart and is always in my mind. She is a teacher, artist, philanthropist and friend. We bonded instantly. Her unwavering passion for helping those less fortunate is at the core of her being.

Beth uses all her creative skills to support a community of women and families who would be considered refugees by our standards. Some are trapped without visas. They have no means for survival. Their children cannot afford to attend school. The only food bank provides food to hundreds of families five nights a week.

Beth works with other women like herself to put twenty kids a year through school from kindergarten to college. She also started a women's cooperative to sell crafts made by some of these mothers. She provides fabric, beads, and materials to several families and the women make an assortment of different craft items. In turn, Beth takes these items to various markets and sells for them, providing the women with an income they would not otherwise have. She teaches them they can be entrepreneurial and self supporting.

Beth has influenced the lives of many women and children through her generous heart. By knowing her, I saw the kind of person I want to be and she became my inspiration for WEMAD, "Women Entrepreneurs Making a Difference."

When things fell apart and I took a hard look at figuring out what I would do, it became obvious. I had to do in Canada what I had been trying to accomplish overseas. I would start WEMAD. Somehow.

I began by looking for a need in my local area that fit my goals. I found more than I expected. My plans for WEMAD expanded. Under the WEMAD umbrella we have:

The Compassionate Companion: A companion care service for seniors that helps families provide loving care for seniors when family members cannot be there. The exponential growth of our senior population and the ailments associated with aging are impacted by a lack of services available to provide care and quality of life for our elders. These concerns are addressed in my upcoming book, *The Companion Advantage, A Guide to Aging Happily Ever After.* The book will be a resource for adult children and families when facing the hard decisions.

Project PURSEverance: A charitable event where filled purses are collected and given out to various charitable organizations that help women in need. In March of this year I partnered with local businesses, Metal Galaxy, Social Games Bistro and the lovely Dorota Ulkowska to hold an event of social games, entertainment and amazing door prizes with the admission being a filled purse. We collected 100 purses which have been distributed.

Workshops: I also have a passion for public speaking and training so I offer workshops in soft skills currently. My goal is to become part of the speaking circuit. I also have a vision where WEMAD holds an annual symposium for women entrepreneurs to come together, collaborating in support of each other's respective businesses to make a difference.

I also see a WEMAD Association in the future, a foundation by the same name and the WEMAD Centre for Hope. Additionally, I am working on two other books: a collection of stories from individuals that live with special needs and a children's book.

With all these massive dreams, I needed a way to earn additional income that was part time. Happily, I was introduced to a new MLM company that made $100 million dollars in one year with one product in one country. Although I had never had an MLM business, nor did I know anything about skin care or accounting, I knew those numbers were over the top and learned they broke every known record. After doing more research, trying the product and learning about the leadership, I found the money to start my own business and discovered I absolutely love it. It's an amazing business model with no overhead, free products and I work at my own convenience, leaving me time to grow WEMAD.

My goal has always been to simply make a positive difference in the lives of people I encounter. The biggest change I would like to see in the world is a shift from the current prevailing negative mindset to one where all things possible.

Bombarded by media reports about the terrible things happening around the world, people adopt that mindset, letting it consume their lives by focusing on the negative everywhere with everyone. Making a positive impact can feel daunting.

So, I started with me. I model the change I want to see by refusing to participate, be sucked in or adapt to this kind of groupthink. I don't watch the news. I don't even have cable. It does not mean I am not informed but rather I choose what I want to be informed about.

I use my time and my talents to bring light and joy to people and the world. I prefer to look at situations and ask, "What small, positive difference can I make?" I start every day by setting an intention of kindness and wellbeing for everyone. Whenever possible I redirect people from a pessimistic perspective to an optimistic one.

WEMAD is the vehicle I use to make this happen.

If you want to see change in the world, you must be that change, to live it and lead by example.

It's important to surround ourselves with people succeeding at doing what we want to do. Find your tribe of successful women and watch how they will pick you up even when you think there is no hope.

Learn from your mentors. If you don't have one, find one.

This is the time of the You Economy and we are forerunners of changing times. Women are unique beings, in that we seem to have a collective soul when it comes to supporting each other. Expose your business, services and vision through networking with other women.

These days, you are always on stage even on social media. You never know who might be listening and what doors may open for you in the most unexpected ways.

Take every opportunity that comes your way to stand up and share your why.

What inspires you? It should connect to your Why. Motivation is easy when the task is finite. However, when you are inspired, that same task can suddenly generate insights and revelations that take you into places you never even considered.

If you are having trouble getting motivated, replace motivation with inspiration.

It's also important to master the mundane, doing the small seemingly inconsequential tasks on a consistent basis over time much like compound interest. I would suggest every entrepreneur read *The Slight Edge* by Jeff Olson to better understand this concept.

It is in the simple, everyday tasks we either succeed or fail.

My joy for life is what gets me up every day. It's all encompassing. Human interaction and the unfolding of new experiences and new people is why I am here and although some experiences may seem negative, I always learn from them. Without the contrast of dark and light, none of us could experience true appreciation.

I spent many years working for corporations and big business with my only goal being the paycheck at the end of the month. However, some years ago I realized I wanted more than that. Money was not my motivation. I longed for purpose, passion and drive; to do something good every day.

Making a difference in someone's life can be as simple as saying hello or smiling at them because we never really know what another person is going through. Every person deserves to feel joy, happiness and love. My strongest desire for my business and life is to help as many people as possible achieve this. If I am to be remembered for anything, I want it to be this.

So, in your life and your business, stay true to yourself, follow your heart and trust your instincts. Don't give meaning to things that do not serve you. Build relationships, not customers.

Wake up every day and find the first thing that makes you smile with joy. Ask yourself, what am I afraid of? Answer the question out loud.

I do this myself, every day.

It's all a choice.

FALL DOWN AND RECOVER

ABOUT CLARA BALL

Clara has always had a heart for travel and considers herself a modern-day gypsy. She loves seeing the world, meeting new people and experiencing everything life offers. Her passion for art, writing, and making a difference in peoples' lives has been an integral part of her life on this journey. As a single mom, balancing work, home life, motherhood, and her passions was not always easy. However, it's time she values because it provides proof that she can be, do or have anything she wants by harnessing the belief and desire to make it happen.

Clara has visited or lived in 26 countries globally and will not stop until she has seen as much of the world as possible. She is the author of the upcoming books *The Companion Advantage, A Guide to Aging Happily Ever After* and *How Much Love Do I Have?* a children's storybook about living between two blended families.

Her dream to make WEMAD (Women Entrepreneurs Making A Difference) the umbrella organization for charitable programs, educational programs, companion care, humanitarian initiatives, and creative expression is the inspiration that lights her gypsy soul on fire every day and the passion behind her purpose.

STEP SIX

Claim

YOUR LEADERSHIP

If you don't like the road you're walking,
start paving another one.
~ Dolly Parton ~

SELF-LEADERSHIP
by Lorraine Crowston

When I was first approached about writing a chapter on leadership, I wondered what I could possibly say that hadn't been covered in thousands of books already in print. By relating it to my own life journey I realized one area of leadership had been overlooked—Self-Leadership. Each person has the ability. Not everyone answers the call.

Here's my path to Self-Leadership.

I was the youngest of six children. I think I won the family jackpot because I had a great childhood. My brothers, sisters and I were blessed with parents who loved us. They loved one another and still do after 67 years of marriage. They raised happy, healthy, well-adjusted children.

My parents expected us to fight our own battles yet live within society's norms and expectations. However, things were changing. Women were no longer stay-at-home moms. They went to work—and worked hard to pay for the car, the house, and for the needs of their family. Single incomes just didn't cut it anymore.

In my case, there was no question as to the path I'd follow; go to school, get a job, get married, buy a house, have kids. There were no entrepreneurs in my family so being my own boss wasn't a consideration, at least not then.

I did the expected. I graduated from college. My Self-Leadership (some may call it independence) led me to move away. I needed to prove I no longer needed to rely on my parents. I was ready for life's grand adventure.

In my first job in a new city, I met my first adult boyfriend. We had a lot of fun but the relationship wasn't really going anywhere. Through him, I met the man I would fall deeply in love with. That relationship would not be a healthy one.

At first, I thought he was perfect. He filled all my "ideal boyfriend" check boxes but after a while I realized something was wrong. This won't be a story about physical or verbal abuse but I'd overlooked the most important check box of all. He didn't love me. He did love my body.

Obviously, it wasn't enough. On top of it all, he insisted we keep our relationship hidden. At first it was innocent enough. We didn't want to hurt the feelings of my first boyfriend, with whom I had parted ways but you'd expect at some point our relationship would become more open. It never happened.

I was the "hider," the mistress he kept tucked away. He wasn't even married! How messed up is that? I was young, deeply in love and stayed with him in the hopes that someday he'd come to love me back. We were together for two years when the relationship unraveled. This happened at the same time as pressures at work increased.

My emotions were taking a beating as was my physical health. I got migraine upon migraine. The nausea I felt at the smell of food made me want to retch. I lost a lot of weight. I only wore pants and long-sleeved shirts so people wouldn't see how thin I'd gotten but they weren't fooled. They thought I had an eating disorder. I, on the other hand, felt as though my world was falling apart as much as my health and emotions were.

I'd been living through my breakup nightmare for a few months. Thankfully, one of my sisters lived nearby and knew what was going on. She invited me over for a visit. When I got to her home I went directly to the washroom. That's where she found me. I was on my knees with my head over the toilet bowl, dry heaves shaking my body as I cried uncontrollably. She held me until I had calmed down.

She very wisely convinced me to pack everything up and to go home to my parents. She knew I couldn't continue. She'd seen the changes and had been alarmed by them. She also knew I was fiercely independent (stubborn) and would have fought to continue with what I was doing. She had waited for the right moment to step in and take charge. It was just in time. I was broken.

She knew staying meant I would see my ex every day. She also knew no office job was worth losing my mind over. I didn't realize it at the time but I had gone down in a giant ball of flames. I had burned out.

I moved back to my childhood home. In my head, I was a complete failure. What grown woman goes home to mommy and daddy? Was I not taught to stand on my own two feet and to fight my own battles? Was I so weak?

My parents were shocked at the condition I arrived in but kept their concern to themselves. Their home was a safe haven. They never asked questions but were always prepared to listen.

It was a very slow recovery. For months, I felt tired all the time. I'd go to bed early only to still be awake at 3:00 am. I caught every cold, throat infection, and flu. The crowning glory was going to the emergency room covered in hives. My mother and I waited for over an hour just to speak to someone. I decided I'd had enough and went over to the nurse's station, my mother at my side, to tell them we were leaving. I suddenly felt very hot, turned to my mother, said "Mom," put my arms around her neck and passed out.

It's amazing how quickly you get attention when you collapse in front of the nurses' station. I woke up, to find myself seated in a wheelchair. I was hyperventilating. They found me a bed but it would still be hours before a doctor came to see me. My mother waited with me.

I knew things were really bad when the nurse asked me to stand up to take my blood pressure. She'd just slipped the cuff around my arm when I threw myself back onto the hospital bed before I passed out again. My blood pressure was so low I couldn't remain standing.

Then the real torture began. She kept pricking me with a needle, attempting find a vein so she could draw blood. At this point, I was crying...so was my mother. That shocked me. I'd never seen my mother cry. Yet here she was standing next to my hospital bed, tears streaming down her face. I knew then, I wasn't suffering alone. I felt terrible that my pain was making my mother cry.

The doctor finally came. For the past few weeks I'd been experiencing a burning sensation in my stomach. The hives were caused when, earlier in the evening, I'd taken ASA for another head ache. This had irritated my already sensitive stomach and caused the hives. The diagnosis was gastritis as a result of all the pain relievers I'd been taking for all the migraines I'd suffered over so many months. Fortunately, it was just a question of a few dietary adjustments, staying away from ASA and time.

Over the course of the next year, I regained my strength and emotional stability. I put the insomnia and gastritis behind me and reflected on what had happened.

It's a shame we don't have foresight. I would have ended the relationship a year sooner before my heart was completely committed. It made me determined it would NEVER happen again. Never again would I let a man treat me badly in a relationship. I would never again be treated as something to be hidden away. Never again would I make myself sick for a job. That was the start of my Self-Leadership.

Self-Leadership Rule: Expect respect.

Self-Leadership Rule: No job is worth getting sick over.

From then on, in every job interview I stated very clearly that if they liked my work there was one basic rule they needed to follow. I told them "I'm happy, I stay. I'm unhappy, I go. If you like my work, keep me happy."

My next boyfriend, who eventually became my husband, was incredibly patient and tenacious. We met through work.

He said he felt it would be best if we didn't tell people about our relationship. That conversation took place as we were strolling through a park on a warm early summer evening. He instantly found himself alone. I'd done an about face and was striding away from him. That certainly surprised him.

When he caught up to me, he grabbed hold of my arm to stop me. Poor bastard! It all came spilling out; what I would and would not ever put up with. Never again! I would not be hidden away like something to be ashamed of. He assured me this wasn't the case. We talked things over and agreed to keeping things discreet for a few weeks but that would be it.

Bless his heart! He took a fair amount of abuse in those first few months. As new situations arose where my "never again" instinct kicked in, he'd ask questions and listen to my answers and explain he'd not meant anything bad by whatever action I had rebelled against until one day he'd had enough. He told me quite bluntly "I'm not him. Stop treating like I am."

He was right. It was the right thing to say. That's when I let him inside my wall of self-preservation and trusted him. It was a part of the Self-Leadership I now applied to my relationships. I let people in after I had determined their character and motives. It turns out to be a pretty good skill. I know the best people!

Self-Leadership rule: Trust is earned.

On the job front, I continued to work for others but in my heart of hearts, I wanted to start a business of my own which I eventually did. In fact, I've started three separate businesses to date. The first was a side business with little risk. I baked cookies and squares to sell to private golf clubs. They were popular for the dessert table at tournaments. The business made a small profit but not enough to quit my day job. I shut it down when my daughter was born and we moved to another city.

It would be sixteen years before I started my next venture. The catalyst was the market crash of 2008. Like so many others, I was laid off from my managerial position. I figured the time was right to go out on my own. Running a sole proprietorship business requires a lot of Self-Leadership. There's absolutely no one to tell you what to do.

I had an idea for a business I thought was a decent concept. I figured I had the right skills and attitude to run it but there were volumes of things I didn't know. It wasn't like the movie Field of Dreams where "If you build it they will come." I built it, but it wasn't selling.

My social media efforts were just starting to have traction when I came across a job posting in my region for a trainer. It was a step back from my management jobs but I wouldn't have to commute. At that point both my husband and I were unemployed and my daughter was about to start at university so I did the responsible thing. I applied and got the job. I set aside my fledgling business and tried my best to quiet my need to be self-employed.

It didn't take long before I felt angry and resentful each day as I sat behind the wheel on my way to work. I did my best to reason and justify being at this job but it all kept coming back to this one question. Why was the entire responsibility for providing for my family on my shoulders? I felt trapped and miserable.

My mental state was suffering. I was constantly exploring other options in my desperate need to get out of my current situation. I went so far as to consider using my husband's and my life savings to purchase a restaurant in another city. It would have taken every penny we had. We wouldn't have had enough for a place to live and I didn't care.

My husband tried to reason with me. I was so angry that he was stopping me from pursuing my dream...any dream that I asked him for a divorce. It absolutely floored him. I did mention that my mental health was suffering.

Fortunately, I immediately came to my senses and recanted. I knew we were better together than apart and I'm glad I realized it in time. After I got better, I spent the following year apologizing for putting him through hell because I'd been so unhappy.

As to the job I hated...I quit. Remember the Self-Leadership rule not to make yourself sick over a job? It was a huge risk. My daughter was at university, my husband held a minimum wage part-time job and I'd quit a job providing a steady pay cheque. I would get no employment insurance because I'd voluntarily left a job even though it was making me emotionally unstable.

143

Self-Leadership rule: Take action.

I was trying to figure out what to do next when I came across an ad for a female entrepreneurs' convention in my area. The price was affordable so I bought a ticket. I'd never been to a networking event...I'd never had to.

I'm not a "half-measures" kinda girl. I wouldn't attend just a small gathering of female entrepreneurs. No way! My first foray had over a hundred attendees.

There were so many things outside of my comfort zone in that one event. First, I hated going alone to a new place where I'd never been before. Second, I hated being in a room full of strangers...no one to talk to. Third, trying to find an empty seat at tables I would have to ask if this seat was taken, risk being told it was and having to scout around for the next available chair. So much rejection!

I was bringing all this baggage with me before I'd even set foot in the room. I found the location without problem. I arrived early and realized the tables were mostly empty. I could sit anywhere. I chose a seat at an empty table and figure the others would have to ask if THEY could join me. Problem solved! From that very first networking event, I met a woman whose services I can't use yet but we've become friends.

Self-Leadership Rule: Live outside of your comfort zone.

My next networking event was just as big. The woman seated next to me told me about a government-funded program designed to help new entrepreneurs. I got as much information as I could and immediately followed up. I applied and was accepted. Not only would I learn the right way to run a business, I would get paid to do it!

I was accepted into the program and met twenty-six like-minded people. I loved every minute I spent learning what to do in my next business venture. I was totally pumped!

Self-Leadership Rule: Always be open to opportunities.

What I learned in the program gave me a solid foundation. However, I felt the structure and tone of the business I'd developed wasn't quite right. I rebranded and modernized the entire concept and launched again. I knew it was no use continuing to work on something that simply wasn't quite right.

Self-Leadership Rule: Adapt and overcome.

My rebranded business still has its hiccups. I wasn't really clear on what I wanted to offer, how to get the message out or how to sell it. The methods taught in my course didn't seem to incorporate any new technology or ideas. My problem became how to use these modern concepts and tools because I had no idea. I was running my business on a line of credit but knew I needed help from experts. I paid people to handle the areas of my business that I couldn't.

Self-Leadership Rule: Know your limitations. Hire experts.

There is one thing I've noticed while working on my rebranding. Whenever my momentum would slow or I felt unsure of what to do next, something always came up at the right time to keep me going. This could be an inexpensive webinar, a speaker at a networking event, advice from a friend, or an idea while having a shower. It happened so often I saw the pattern.

I should tell you, after spending over 15 years in Information Technology, I wasn't really into "New Age" ideals. However, there were so many happy coincidences, I couldn't

CLAIM YOUR LEADERSHIP

ignore the obvious. The cosmos, universe, God, whatever it was, wanted me to succeed.

Self-Leadership Rule: Keep an open mind.

I could go on and on with any number of other Self-Leadership Rules but it would fill a book and I only have one chapter. The point isn't so much that you must follow mine but to create and follow your own Self-Leadership Rules.

Find what serves you best and live a good life.

ABOUT LORRAINE CROWSTON

Lorraine Crowston is a Wellness Strategist, Nutritional Therapist, and Certified Coach Practitioner with a Certificate in Sports and Exercise Nutrition and in Adult Education. She helps her clients discover the triggers that make them eat and act in ways that do not serve them.

Her passion is helping people to achieve emotional and physical health in fun and easy ways.

She produced, directed and hosted her own webTV program called Let's Face It. She is a sought after and engaging speaker and the author of *The Devil's Food Cake Made Me Do It.*

Lorraine has worked as a cook, chef and restaurant manager. She has spent the bulk of her career in the Information Technology field where she held positions as an instructor, trainer, manager of professional services and project manager. It was after leaving the IT field that she chose to pursue her passion and launched her practice as a Wellness Strategist. She understands first-hand the stress and strain of modern living and helps others achieve balance and health in their hectic lives.

Lorraine is busy in her business but makes time to relax. Her main activities are handcrafts that she does while watching television. Her favorite (what she terms as her addiction) is spinning fibres and wool into yarn.

She loves to play golf, hike, travel and enjoys meeting so many wonderful people.

She and her husband live on the north shore of Lake Ontario with their dog and two cats. They are the proud parents of wonderful adult daughter.

GROW INTO LEADERSHIP
by Dianne Najm

Nothing is absolute. Everything changes,
everything moves, everything revolves,
everything flies and goes away.
~ Frida Kahlo ~

I believe that nothing is absolute and without change, there is no growth. Most of us would stay in our comfort zone because it feels safe. Change invites the unknown. However, with change comes innovation, creativity and another level of confidence and leadership.

These days I look back in amazement and see how far I've come. Even though the fear of change was present, I still moved forward.

I'm lucky to be surrounded by people who want to support me and elevate me no matter what I am doing. The first female in my family to get a college degree, I didn't follow the norms of marriage and family. Instead, I worked outside the home.

I started out as a social worker. My clients were children and women who suffered abuse. To empower women and help children heal from those hurts was my passion

I spent 20 years as a social worker before becoming an entrepreneur. About that time, I learned the truth about absolutes and change.

I accidentally fell into the entrepreneurial world when I launched PhotoPAD, a Facebook app for consumers to share photos in albums with their Facebook friends. When I reached 250k users, I won a "Mom of the Business Award." The press release announcing that award led to businesses on Facebook using our app. That then led to further discussions and the launch of PhotoPAD for Business on the web.

While I feel I've always been part of the change I want to see, both personally and professionally, PhotoPAD allowed me to help other women and subsequently their families in ways I couldn't imagine in my 20 years as a social worker. My success as an entrepreneur gave me more reach and allows me to create more impact than I could have achieved in my former profession.

My core values and my passion to be of service to women and their families continues to be reflected in how I give back to the community around me. I serve on the board of Olive Crest, an organization that helps children heal from abuse. In the entrepreneurial realm, I mentor women, particularly young women, on how to open doors as well as support other women on their journey to succeed. One way I do that is by connecting them with the resources they need.

If I could sit down with you as a female entrepreneur, here's the advice I'd offer.

First and foremost, STEP BOLDLY into your role as Leader whether it is your own business or your current role in a corporation.

These days, more women are accepting a leadership role. We are leaving the corporate world and starting our own businesses because we know we are capable leaders. In 2009, 9.5%

startups had at least one female founder. By 2014 that rate had almost doubled to 18%.

As the leader, the vision and ideas belong to you, so it is you who make it fail or succeed. Accept that responsibility and lead with confidence, knowing that failure or success is part of the process. The more you accept this, the more you will grow.

Keep your vision clear and stay on course by empowering both yourself and your team. While the responsibility is yours, you don't need to do it all yourself. Draw on the strengths of your team and you all succeed.

Show up for meetings and don't ask where to sit. Take the seat at the head of the table. Be present and attentive. Always know you are the leader.

Embracing fear and uncertainty is a must for navigating the Leader's Journey and to show others the way. Keeping this as part of your mindset helps with clarity and focus. When you start pushing through problems and find the inner confidence to lead, invaluable lessons are learned.

I would not have believed this when I was younger because most of us were taught failure is "bad" and to be avoided. However, the lessons it provides make it a confidence builder as well as a humbling experience. One of the lessons I learned is that, at the end of each day, I focus on affirmations or the positive things that happened that day.

Second, be authentic.

To "be you" is a powerful attribute for a successful leader. I don't waver in what I stand for and believe in so I am authentic in this way.

The hardest lesson I learned as an entrepreneur is that not everyone has the same values and interest in helping others. It's hard for me to understand women who do not help other women but instead, are willing to trample on them to claim the spotlight.

I also find it difficult to accept that after all these years there is still pay inequality and scarce opportunities at senior levels for women. This is sustained by a belief pattern on the part of both genders that holds back women in the workplace. Many think this will change when men change but I believe it takes all of us. As women entrepreneurs, I feel it's important for us to support the success of other women as well as those men who want to be part of the solution.

My vision includes women standing side by side with men where gender does not make a difference in deciding a senior level position and the pay reflects the skill.

I also look forward to the day when women do not feel they need to label themselves "BossBabe," "Kickass Women," "WomenLeader." These kinds of labels trouble me because I believe when women feel the need to use them, it places them below their counterpart.

Because of that, I have the privilege as the CEO of Photo-PAD for Business to feature female business owners in photo stories I share on my social media, blogs and more. My business allows me to promote and spotlight their talents.

Whenever I give a presentation, I share my journey of becoming a leader, founder and CEO of a tech company with a non-tech background. I tell them how PhotoPAD for Business challenges me through my multiple roles, leading the tech team, making tough decisions, and always moving forward. I explain how it has been an amazing journey, filled with both failures and successes. If my story inspires other women to take the leap, make the change and gain the confidence to move forward, then I know I'm living my purpose.

Find your authentic purpose and let it guide the impact you create with your business.

CLAIM YOUR LEADERSHIP

Third, growth happens as a leader when you stay the course and allow yourself to change when it's required.

Assess all feedback and move forward when it's needed. To discover the right feedback, choose a role model to emulate. Perhaps more than one.

Throughout my journey, I've encountered many role models, both in my life and in my business. It would be difficult, if not impossible to name just one. My list includes professors, mentors and coaches who have been impactful. My parents and relatives motivated me as they were successful entrepreneurs. My grandparents emigrated here from Greece to start several businesses.

I'm inspired by looking to those who maintained strength and displayed unwavering courage, especially in the face of opposition. I'm drawn to women in leadership positions who believed in and changed the lives of those around them for the better such as Benazir Bhutto, who stood for women's freedom; Sheryl Sandberg who advises women to "Lean in" and Mother Teresa for "giving so much to all humanity." These are just some examples. There are many others.

Looking forward twenty years, I want to be known, as those women were, for doing the right thing, living my values and giving back on all levels. It is my lifestyle now and always has been. Whether you view me as a success or failure, I am always consistent. Anything I have done has been through growth and evolving into my authenticity.

It's who I am that makes me the leader I am today.

Besides your role models, gather a tribe of people around you who are supportive and will lift you as you climb. I am grateful for my family and friends and feel lucky to have them by my side. In addition, I'm grateful to all the mentors that came forward to help me on this entrepreneurial journey! I would not be here today if not for all of them.

I am blessed by God, I have my faith and HE has my back. That belief keeps me motivated to move forward and be the change I want to see in this world.

So perhaps that is my final advice to you.

Express gratitude for change and the people who are on your side as you step into your leadership role. Then be the change YOU want to see in this world.

ABOUT DIANE NAJM

Diane Najm is the CEO & Founder of PhotoPad. After practicing Social Work for over twenty years, Diane leapt into the entrepreneurial space when she launched her first product PhotoPad, a consumer photo app on Facebook in 2010 and PhotoPad for Business in 2016.

Her passion and leadership continues to empower women to succeed in business through providing resources and connections. She serves on the Board of Directors to *Women in Wireless* and *Women in Tech*. As a Past Director of Founder Institute and a mentor to start-ups, she was invited to the Seattle White House Digital Tech Summit. She regularly speaks about entrepreneurship and leadership. Her credits include Microsoft, Women Who Code, Women in Tech Seattle and Vancouver and Startup Weekend in which her teams have come in first and second place.

She received the 2015 Woman of the Year in Business Award, 2012 Mom of the Year Business Award and 2012 Ambassador to the Children Community Award. She continues to do philanthropy work for women and children of abuse and serves on the Board of Trustees for Olive Crest.

PASS IT ON
by Charity Schaefer

My spirit is unbridled. My mind is strong. Loyalty flows strongly through my veins. The people I have the pleasure of meeting during this journey on Earth I hope see me as a friend—a friend in deed.

My name is Charity Schaefer. I was born a Georgia peach but raised primarily a Bluegrass girl in the great state of Kentucky. I have heard it said some people are born with a silver spoon in their mouth. I like to say I had a wooden one.

However, the hardest lesson I've had to learn is that I am enough. I learned that lesson through the difficulties I faced in my life.

It was in the moments I felt my lowest that carved and created my character today. As I watched others around me fall victim to their circumstances, I witnessed potential and ambition turn to stone and sadness. I chose a different path and I'm grateful for the challenges I faced growing as a child.

The oldest of four siblings, things were not always easy but I know my parents love me. Some of the most amazing lessons and even some of the traits I carry today I gained from those experiences and my family. I learned to call adversity my friend. She and I know one another well. They say your pain is your power. I believe this hundred percent. While some would consider these difficulties to be tombstones they became my stepping stones.

Throughout my life I realized there are two roads. One is playing the victim and the other is finding the lesson and growing from it. I am thankful I opted for the latter of the two. It has been a long road of growth.

Due to an unstable childhood home, I recall sleeping in an orphanage hall in my pre-teen years. Later, my siblings and I found ourselves split half and half in the foster care system. In my twenties and homeless, I hit rock bottom.

I realized I needed to make some changes. I would not allow my circumstances to define me. Rather, I would rise above them. I would create my reality.

Uncertain, scared and the mother of two beautiful little girls, I signed a contract with the United States Army and set out weeks later to begin my Basic Training Boot Camp.

Two years later and after a deployment in Afghanistan, I was thankful but frustrated with the lack of time freedom I had with my girls and my husband. At that time, I was given the opportunity to start my own business. It has been a stepping stone towards my calling that continues to unfold.

Today, the change I want to see in the world is women stepping into their own greatness. In my perfect world, each woman claims her crown and then crowns more women.

As Gandhi said, the best way to create this change is simply by being the change. Every day, be an example. I know there's a light planted purposefully inside of me. I embrace my uniqueness and enjoy encouraging women to do the same thing. My purpose and commitment is to be that change I want to see.

Hard work, grit, determination and laughter are the DNA of my life's work. All my life experiences made me stronger. I am a stronger wife. I am stronger mother. I am a stronger friend. I am stronger woman.

They are the foundation of my success in business.

Let me assure you, I'm not perfect. I've been guilty of running from my own potential. Too many times to count, I second guessed myself because hiding is easy. There have been moments I literally peeled myself off the floor to go out and face the day.

However, when you stay hidden you can't do much to help and that's selfish. I learned the importance of believing in yourself even when it feels like you're the only one.

Frequently, I fell prey to other people's opinions, allowing them to shape me and my belief system. This left me frustrated and angry. I wore many masks and it was exhausting.

However, when you see or hear me today I am always unmasked. I wear my crown proudly and empower other women to do the same thing. I'm creating a global tribe of *come-with-us* girls versus *look-at-me* girls. I want women to know it's okay to be vulnerable and strong at the same time.

My goal is to inspire other women to take their own masks off.

Too many women with huge potential are content to sit quietly on the sidelines. As my own business grew, it became very clear no one was going to do it for me (and they won't do it for you). I focus inwards on my potential and do what I can to manifest that capability on the outside. I do that as an example of change to the women around me so they rightfully take and wear their crowns.

Empowering women isn't something I take lightly. As women, we should be lighting each other's candles rather than blowing them out. Together we shine brighter. We need to keep passing on the light.

Seriously, no more throwing other women down the stairs. Let's just not.

Today, I help other women create successful businesses. These women show up and apply themselves to improving their life and business every day. It's a culture I refer to as the "boss, love, and shine" tribe in my business.

Actually, I don't work with women. I work with Queens and I want each of them to feel that to their core. I want them to embrace that mentality and run sky high with it while remaining humble enough to help their sisters along.

We are in this together. Our talents are more powerful together. I have no time for "mean girls." Seriously, I am just sick of that attitude. I refuse to be a part of it and I am not going to empower it.

My advice to you reading this is to grab your opportunities and take more risks. If it's scary or uncomfortable, go for it anyway. You will never know if you don't try and you will always learn something. Always.

Look inside. Identify who and what you stand for. Then stand up and roar. Commit to living out your purpose. Cultivate those seeds. Stick around for the harvest.

Love your great qualities and strengthen your weaknesses. There will always be people who try to knock you off your beautiful stallion but love yourself so much, believe in yourself so much, that it just won't matter.

Decide. Don't wait for permission. Ignore the doubters and naysayers. They will attempt to dim your light. Don't allow them to define your truth. Those types aren't going anywhere. Rather, choose to forgive them while you go on to be awesome!

There will be days you won't feel like stepping out and embracing your power. The advice I offer (and follow personally) is "Just do it anyway."

The most trying days require us to step up in an even bigger way. When I feel tested I look for one thing I can achieve that day and do it. The process of fulfilling that one task and checking it off makes a huge difference. It recharges my power to get on with whatever else must be done for another day.

Today, the advice I would give to my younger self would be to stop worrying so much. This has been one of the biggest challenges for me. I allowed worry to steal my joy. There were so many moments I missed the greatness of the present because I worried to much about the future.

A mentor told me once if it would not matter in five years do not give more than five minutes of attention to it. Since then, I've learned everything really does work out. Life is such a gift. Embrace every moment. If you spend your days worrying you rob yourself and steal from those around you.

I have two wishes.

Twenty years from now, I hope I provided an example for my two amazing daughters, helping them to achieve their maximum potential. With the correct mindset, I want them to know that anything is possible with enough belief and action.

My other dream is to leave a legacy of nurturing thousands of women worldwide and helping them reach their potential. I want this to happen because I have been loving, kind, real and raw today.

People have grown weary of false masquerades and continuous games. The days of sitting quietly on the sidelines in pearls, a feathered hat and a tailored dress are done. Roll your sleeves up, ladies. It's time for women to show up and shine through. To rule as Queens.

Purchase all the shares from YOU, Inc. UP your belief in yourself. If that means declaring at the top of your lungs self-proclaimed mantras in the mirror daily, DO IT!

I do.

ABOUT CHARITY SCHAEFER

Despite a life path that led through orphanages, foster care and homelessness, Charity Schaefer has an upbeat and positive perspective on life.

Today she lives in Santa Rosa Beach, Florida with her two amazing daughters and husband. Her hobbies include serving and volunteering in her community with the Junior League and spontaneous travel to add to her family's life adventures.

Her vision leads her to inspire other woman to keep climbing and be strong on a daily basis in her business and relationships. She models for them a change in perspective that allows them to see that the word impossible contains the words (I'm)possible.

You can connect with Charity through:
www.charityschaefer.com

STEP SEVEN

IT'S *Bigger* THAN YOU

What you do makes a difference, and you have to decide what kind of difference you want to make.
~ Jane Goodall ~

ACTS OF KINDNESS
by Candace Maruk

Before I was an entrepreneur I was a stay-at-home mom. My husband worked in Egypt and was gone overseas for a month and then home for a month. We had a 2-year-old son at the time so I quit my job because it was too much to handle everything on my own alone.

Then three years later we had another little boy while my husband still commuted back and forth to Egypt. However, right around then a lot of things were going on over there so he decided to come back to Canada to work. I needed to find something to fill the financial void this change created.

Because we had two young children, working outside the home didn't feel like an option for me. For that reason, I joined a network marketing company the first day it came to Canada in 2015. I've never looked back.

While it was a journey I originally took on to help my family financially, the company's model and their values completely changed my life. Part of that stems from their contributions of both money and product to a charity near and dear to my own heart—The Ronald McDonald House—as well as a charity called "Girl Talk" which supports young girls, ages 9 and up, in many positive ways.

I believe it makes us better people not to just think about ourselves but to think of others so it was a natural fit for me to align with a company that desires to pay it forward. They exemplify everything I seek to be. So, the first advice I want to share with you as an entrepreneur would be to get clear on what's important to you and find a way to reflect that in your own business.

When I joined this company I also joined a community of shared values. Each month they ask us to focus on a single value. For instance, this month it was "Courageous." And, while I profit from the products, the encouragement and support also benefit me. I see my business as an outlet to do good.

My second piece of advice to you would be to find (or create) your own community of people who share your values. It's no secret that we're more powerful together.

I didn't realise how empowered I'd feel just from being in this business. Not only that, it got me out of the house and gave me the confidence to stand up in front of a group of people. There was a time when there was no way I'd even walk into a room if there wasn't someone by my side.

I've gained a lot of Vitamin "C" through my business: Connection, Courage and Confidence.

My business gives me the time, freedom and resources to take on a lot of volunteer work. I started that journey a long time ago when I was young. It has become my outlet, like other people have hobbies.

I guess you could say my hobby is giving back. It makes my heart warm and fills my cup. It fills me with enjoyment when I can make someone else's day better, even when it's just thanking someone for something they've done.

When I turned 31, we had just the one son, who was three that year. As part of my birthday celebration, my son and I performed 31 random acts of kindness. For instance, we gave the men who picked up our garbage cold drinks and treats on an extremely hot day. They rewarded us with huge smiles and now they wave every time they come by to pick up the garbage. They never forgot the kindness we showed them.

Because of my birthday celebration, I won the Female Citizen of the Year award for 2013 here in our little town of Stettler. That was a huge honor because in our area it's typically the older generation who receives this award. It was humbling to think they chose me.

My boys are six and two now. My goal is to teach my children to look up to yourself and take care of yourself but this is a big world. If you can spread a little bit of kindness by doing one small random act of kindness at a time you will brighten more lives than you will ever know about. Plus, you're not just doing good for other people; you're also doing good for our own spirit.

My husband is a firefighter and he did the biggest stair climb in the world—775 feet. Our 6-year-old decided he wanted to help. We chose a tote from my business, filled it full of camping stuff and sold tickets. Our son even did all the videos and stuff himself. He hustled hard and sold 162 tickets, raising $810 for his dad's stair climb team. An experience like that is confidence building (and if you build a child's confidence they can do anything).

My vision of success includes a kinder world. I've always felt that while you're here you might as well make a positive impact on the world.

If I could change one thing about our world it would be have people think more about others. At least once in your day, do one small gesture for someone else. It doesn't have to be anything huge. If each of us did just one act of kindness each day what a change we'd see around us. Imagine the ripple effect!

I've used my business to do small things for other people, like donating products. We recently asked customers to help us create "Love Bins" for seniors in a lodge or nursing home. Those who chose to, sponsored a bin for $25. I filled it with things seniors could use and delivered them.

The most empowering lesson of my life happened when I was young. I didn't have the easiest childhood and found myself on my own when I was 16. That's probably when my volunteerism started.

I was part of 4H and had to do a project centered on community service. I chose to help a little boy in my area who was receiving a liver transplant. His family needed financial help to go back and forth to the hospital.

I organized a bake sale that contributed $500 to help them out. After that, I thought "This is a really good feeling. I can do this and I can help other people." Everything stemmed from that project. It taught me that even when things seem hard, other people have it a lot worse. That boy's need made me look beyond my own need.

Don't get me wrong. I'm human. I get discouraged occasionally. After all, I'm toilet training a 2-year-old right now.

What discourages me the most however, is someone telling me something can't be done. Although truthfully, I don't know if that's really about discouragement. I'm stubborn. So, when someone says something is impossible, I tend to go the other way to try and make it happen. I like proving the naysayers wrong. I believe I can do anything I put my mind to. I wake up every single day with the thought.

In the end, I'd like to be remembered for encouraging someone else to do something kind. I want people to talk about how I modelled kindness and how it inspired them to do something they may have felt was beyond them.

I'm not naïve. I know some people may question how kindness translates into a business success. I'd tell them kindness is what business should be about. After all, being kind to customers is good customer service. So, if kindness isn't one of their business values, I'd say they're probably doing something wrong. It certainly works for me.

Find your heroes and role models and emulate them. My real-life hero is my husband. He's such a go-getter, he inspires me every day. I look at him and think about all the things he's done with his life and just go WOW.

My celebrity hero would be Ellen DeGeneres. She's so kind and humble. Yes, she does things because businesses are promoting her but she also gives from the goodness of her heart. Her genuineness shines through.

I could also name many everyday people like friends and relatives that I admire. Frankly, heroes are everywhere. You just need to look around.

I have a pretty darn good life. I'm thankful for it and my husband and my boys are the ones who make it so great. It's always been my dream to be a mom and wife, to go to school and be a volunteer. I can honestly say I'm living my dream. Not everyone can say that so it's one more thing I'm grateful for.

If I could go back in time to give my younger self advice I'd tell myself, "Be more confident. Believe in your ability to do things on your own. Just believe more in yourself and be more outgoing."

Good advice for anyone in business.

My final advice to you as a business woman would be "Never give up. Keep on keeping on."

When you wonder if you're ever going to "get it," think about the people whose lives you may change. It might not even be as a result of using your product or service but simply because of a conversation you have with them. Believe in yourself and your value.

And oh, yes...be kind.

ABOUT CANDACE MARUK

Candace Maruk holds many titles, but the ones most dear to her heart are firefighter's wife, Mommy to two boys and business owner. She's proud of the person she's become and looks forward to each day. She teaches others, "Do what makes you happy. Be loyal to those you love and spread kindness whenever possible."

She is also a director with 31 Gifts with a team of 47 and growing.

In a world filled with incredible people and undeniable potential, she doesn't plan on sitting back and wasting a second of it.

IT'S BIGGER THAN YOU

FIND YOUR VISION AND PURPOSE
by Cindy Chrenek

One morning at 2 a.m., I decided to drop out of college and go kick some butt in the workforce. I started in retail and eventually worked up to management.

I was young. I was successful. I knew what it meant to have a vision, set goals and work hard at creating the life I wanted. I was breaking all kinds of records. I felt irreplaceable.

I never watched the clock and always went above and beyond. As I developed people to be promoted, I truly thought it was okay to work 60 to 80 hours a week. I bought into the idea that by trading my life for recognition, I would somehow arrive in my happy place.

Fast forward 10 years to a Monday afternoon at 4 p.m. They fired me.

To say I felt embarrassed and devastated would be an absolute understatement. I still remember the terrible feeling in the pit of my stomach.

My one thought was "What would people think?" I needed to find something fast because I didn't want to face the humiliation of telling my friends and family. All I focused on was replacing my income as quickly as I could because I didn't want anyone to know I was out of work. I also knew that never, ever again would I give someone else the power to take away my income and self esteem in a single moment.

All good reasons for me to build a business through network marketing then run hard towards my goal of success. Right from the start, I made great money and I quickly fell in love with the whole process.

Here was an industry I hadn't even known existed before I lost my job but it was where I would build the career of my dreams. I chose my hours and my holidays. When I had children, I could stay at home with them. Having control over my time and no limits on my income is the most amazing feeling in the world. Finally, I lived for me!

I also quickly achieved financial success. However, I wanted to live with a sense of purpose so I began to look around for a better fit with my values. I looked for a business I could succeed at AND be passionate about.

A woman whom I have tremendous of respect for, advised me that "the biggest mistake a rookie in network marketing can make is to ignore when it's time to move on and find a new company." That was probably the most important advice I ever received because if I had not taken it seriously I wouldn't be where I am today.

In 2010, I found my dream company. I always wanted to travel but used the excuse I didn't have the money. Now my new business allowed me to travel, make money and have fun. I vacationed at business events with friends every three months which added a tremendous amount of joy to my life. I can't even explain how awesome it feels to lose count of how many times I laugh in a day.

However, despite my amazing experiences something was still missing from my life. That "something" began to gel as I listened to other people's stories about Voluntour service trips. As they shared their life-affirming experiences, their

IT'S BIGGER THAN YOU

171

stories and emotions engaged my heart. However, I didn't follow up and continued my path of business-building.

Then something happened to shift my trajectory.

Just before a family vacation to Puerto Vallarta, we learned I was pregnant with our third child. Trust me, I would not have planned a trip to Mexico if I'd known I was expecting.

So, try to imagine this...I'm in Mexico with some of my closest friends at an all-inclusive, 4 Diamond Resort. The location is beautiful, the weather great. It's a picture-perfect vacation, worthy of postcards.

My husband and I are the only ones who know I'm pregnant so for that entire week I made it look like I enjoyed my non-alcoholic beverages. I didn't let the cat out of the bag.

Extremely nauseous, I honestly didn't want to be there despite the fact I'm the type of girl who likes to have a good time. My heart just wasn't in it. Was it my hormones? Perhaps the fact I felt like a bloated pig? I just wanted to go home.

On the last day of the trip, everything changed.

That's when I took part in my first service excursion day at a community center called Entre Amigos in San Pancho. It was an eye-opening experience and shifted something inside of me.

I found my vision and purpose.

That was the first time I knew I'd partnered with the right company because volunteering is the core value of our company. We even offer vacations centered around giving back. On that trip, I felt what it was like to be in a third world country and potentially change the lives of others.

Initially I was shocked by how difficult life is there and the contrast between my life and theirs. Everything is recycled and reused there. I felt mortified thinking about how much I waste. I was blown away by how much I had and took for granted while these people had so little but knew happiness.

It's not like I didn't know life was like this but it's different when you see it and feel it. You only truly "get it" when you're immersed in the situation.

I spent my first afternoon of service with one of my best friends, painting chairs. The people were so appreciative for our support. I'm happy to report that even though I felt like throwing up and my pants were tight and uncomfortable, I had the time of my life.

After my first experience, I wanted to jump right in and do more, but life sometimes doesn't give you everything you want. I found being in business and pregnant with my third was more challenging than with my first child. Then I had my baby and because of a slowdown in the economy, I lost my motivation and focus.

Almost two years passed before I took part in another trip with a service excursion component. My spirits were once again lifted with excitement when we decided to go back to Puerto Vallarta and take advantage of another opportunity to give back. This time my eight-year-old son was involved.

It became a small obsession of mine to make this day perfect for him. I knew this could have a major impact on him even as an adult and that excited me. This opportunity would give him an understanding many children will never know.

Before we left, he collected fifty pounds of school supplies from his peers and my colleagues to hand deliver to the children at Entre Amigos. Then he took it one step further and had his grade two class write pen pal letters to the children in Spanish.

He experienced what it's like to do something good for someone else. I especially loved this because he also gave other people an opportunity to contribute and support this event.

Kids have everything today. The toys…. Ahhh, the toys. Most kids today can't imagine what life was like even just fifteen years ago. These days it seems our children just expect things and want more all the time. We as parents have the power to change that.

I want to raise my children to serve others. I want my children to feel compassion, appreciation and gratitude. What I love about travel are the wonderful memories we create that last for a lifetime. What I love about combining travel with a service element are creating memories *and* positive change, not just for the communities we visit but also in ourselves and our children.

If I could jump ahead twenty years I would love to hear how my story changed other families. I'd like to think that, when parents learned about our Voluntour trips, it inspired them to give their children the same opportunity. I'd also like to hear how they showed their children to give at home as well as on vacation.

Our children are the future and they need experiences that make them feel a part of something positive. They also need a break from technology to create those memories. Family vacations are the perfect time to do this.

Take a day out of your vacation to serve the community center in San Pancho or participate in building bottle schools in Guatemala. Take on a project in Kenya or work with orphanages in Thailand, Bali and Zimbabwe or simply find a need closer to home. The list is endless and the possibilities to serve are always available.

I'm so fortunate to be able to use my business to help people experience travel as well as service on a global level, one trip at a time.

The best advice I can offer you as a woman in business is to find the right fit for your passion then align yourself with great people. Build relationships and always support other women in business. The climb is the same no matter what your product or service may be. Then use your business to give back. Once you decide it's not just about the money, you will uncover your sense of purpose.

Once you find it, you will be unstoppable.

IT'S BIGGER THAN YOU

ABOUT CINDY CHRENEK

Cindy Chrenek is a network marketing professional with over a decade experience. Prior to that, she worked in the corporate world for two of Canada's largest retail companies. She achieved many awards for developing employees and hitting sales milestones and was handpicked for several projects during her retail management career.

Making the transition to network marketing was not a difficult one for her as she has a heart to serve others. Cindy built teams numbering into the thousands and other major achievements. Passionate about the travel industry, she has aligned herself with World Ventures, the world's leading travel network marketing company. During this time, she has been on over thirty flights taking part in volunteer projects both abroad and at home.

She thrives on finding the balance between being a stay-at-home mom while building a home-based business. Her experiences have revealed a passion for showing other women how to be successful in the industry.

STEP EIGHT

THE *next* STEP

*This journey has always been about
reaching your own other shore no matter
what it is, and that dream continues.*
~ Diana Nyad ~

TELL YOUR STORY
by Aprille Janes

Welcome! You've arrived at the end of the beginning.

When Gandhi advised us to "Be the change" he was saying all change starts with us and reaches out from there, like ripples on the water.

Reflecting that approach, our first book in the *Divas That Care* series looks at business as a vehicle for personal growth and change. The next "ripple in our pond" will be stories from women using their business as a vehicle for world change. Women just like you.

If you're like most entrepreneurs, you love the work you do and the people you serve. You know you provide valuable services and products your clients and customers truly need. Because you're reading this book, it's safe to assume you also want to effect positive change in the world using your business as a vehicle.

The next step in your own journey may be to share your story to inspire others. If you've looked at successful thought leaders and dreamt of joining their ranks, we can help. You're just as talented, capable, and are up to big stuff, right?

Most of those thought leaders have a memorable story. A great story can open hearts and changes a conversation completely. Everyone wants to grow but we don't want to be preached at.

Story changes everything.

So, how do you tell a great story? Before I answer that, let me tell you a little bit about me and why I feel I'm uniquely qualified to write this chapter.

I have always loved creativity. I ran my own art studio when I was in my 20s before I went back to school to train in the field of technology. After graduation, I entered the corporate world and became a consultant for all kinds of companies from small businesses to Fortune 500s. I traveled and had a wonderful time.

I also dreamt of being both a writer and a coach/consultant for more passionate, world-changing entrepreneurs, so I eventually let corporate consulting in 2003 to pursue my vision. I was quickly published in many local magazines, had a regular gig in a major Toronto newspaper in the careers section and I started writing fiction. I began with short stories, won some awards, and eventually taught creative writing.

As a natural progression from the teaching of writing, I wrote a book called *Gulp Fiction* to help people who were just getting into fiction writing. People who had never written anything had a lot of success with the book, because as a certified coach I used my training to encourage their creativity.

Eventually, I noticed people talking about story in the business world, and as a business coach who loves a good story, that *really* excited me. Since then I've facilitated workshops, coached my clients on how to use stories in their businesses and helped entrepreneurs change their entire success trajectory with this work.

I guess you could say I'm passionate about story and what it can do in this world. The entrepreneurs I work with are truly shaking up the status quo, and story is one of their most valuable tools. It has a two-fold effect, helping them succeed AND share their message of change.

BUSINESS DIVAS THAT CARE

Stories create empathy and build trust. Stories also ignite action. If all people needed were facts and stats, there would be no hunger, global warming, health issues, or poverty. But when a story makes something feel personal and touches our emotions, we get moving and change happens.

When I taught creative writing, one of the things I always said to my students was, "Don't apologize for writing fiction because the one thing that has always changed the world is a good story."

As I said, people don't transform their lives and society because of facts and arguments and stats. We change because someone touches our heart. And when we can connect our heart to what we need to do, we get *into motion*. Story creates *action*. Story *connects* people.

As you consider sharing your story, one of the most important things to remember (because you may be a little nervous at this point) is: *you do not need to be creative to put a story together.*

Our logical brain wants the world to make sense. It's our logical brain telling us stories continuously about what's going on around us. In fact, you could say we live our lives in narrative. Have you ever made up a story about why something was happening? Somebody cut you off in traffic and you've got this whole rrr-rrr-rrrr going on about them? It's your inner chatter, right?

That's your left-brain, not the creative right-side. So, story in the truest sense is not *a creative act.* Making up a fictional story? That's a creative act. But *telling* stories is not, because it's our logical brain just trying to make order and sense out of our lives.

If you ask most people to name all nine U.S. Supreme Court Justices, they'll probably have to ask Google. *(Aren't two of them named Anthony? What? Antonin? Are you sure?)*

181

Ask the same people to name nine Disney characters, and they'll laugh as they rattle 43 characters off the top of their heads. The musically inclined will probably even give you a little song and dance from their favorite for your trouble. That, my friends, is the power of storytelling.

Stories become memorable. Stories *stick* with us. Stories touch our hearts before making a pathway to our brains.

It's also important to understand what a story is NOT.

Stories are not Power Point slides or an instruction book. Too many people try to create change by prescribing "Well, first you do this, and then you do that, and then you do the next thing." That's not a story. Just because something seems to have a beginning, middle, and end, does not make it a story. Rather, it's more like ordering people around and they tend to dig in their heels.

And finally, story is not emotional manipulation. It's not arm-twisting or guilt-tripping. People worry using a story might be manipulative because we *are* talking about touching people's hearts and there is a reason for concern because we've all experienced this type of manipulation.

What makes a story rise above manipulation is *your intent*.

If you're out there to put a guilt trip on somebody to compel them to take a specific action because you've wrung out their heart, that's emotional manipulation. However, if you tell that same story with the intent of "What in my experience or someone else's experience is going to help you?" then you're creating a connection that *deepens their understanding* of a problem and makes them *emotional available* to a solution.

For instance, I mentioned earlier I had an art studio when I was in my 20s. When I was about 28, a recession hit our area, and I've got to tell you, an art studio is a luxury item. Unemployment in our area zoomed to over 20%, and art was the first thing to get dropped from personal budgets.

Customers simply stopped coming almost overnight and within a month, our studio was history. We had two very young children and we had just lost everything. The only thing left was our furniture because it wasn't worth enough to sell and the bank allowed us to buy back our car. That was all "the stuff" we had left to rebuild our life.

But you know, we felt lucky. We were young, we had each other, our health and our children. My husband found a very good job in his field in a nearby city. The kids and I soon joined him. I went back to school and we recovered.

When I became a business coach, I was afraid to tell that story for a very long time because I thought, "How can my clients trust me if I say, 'Oh, by the way, I lost a business in my 20s?'"

Out of all my experiences, I thought that one should be swept under the rug. It wasn't until I saw the value in what I had learned and realized it might also serve my clients that I began sharing it. To my surprise, my clients responded by trusting me more. The lesson they told me they took from my story was this:

"It's the fear of risk holding me back from my dreams. I keep telling myself I could lose everything but Aprille lost everything and survived. She's right. It's all just stuff. Should the worst happen, I will recover. The only thing I can't replace are the people I love and my health."

So, my story, which could easily be a heart-wringer, is used with integrity in service of others. It helps them see their fear is so much bigger than the real risks they are taking. It helps them move past their fear of loss. It gives them hope and shows them what's really at stake—their dreams.

And *that* is the power of story.

THE NEXT STEP

We don't identify with the "big picture" as human beings. We need the personal. We need to be able to hone in on one person, one activity, one story that gives a face to whatever it is we do.

Psychologists have proven we make decisions with our emotions, by the way, and not our heads. Our heads *justify it*, but our hearts decide. It's not manipulation but the way we are wired as human beings.

But why? What about our wiring connects so readily with story? A recent graduate university study proved that stories activate a hormone in our body called oxytocin, which is also known as the love hormone. So, when we say we *love* stories, I mean, we really *LOVE* stories.

This same hormone creates the bond a mother has for her newborn child, and it explains why stories help us bond to each other and create a sense of community. If I say to you, "Let me tell you a story," your body starts to release oxytocin, and mine too, so we create this relationship between us initiated by the story.

There have been several studies done, notably one at Washington University, where researchers put people in an MRI machine to track what was going on in their brains. First, they read the participants a series of stats and bullet points and only one portion of the brain activated—the language portion.

We already know if someone gives us a big long list of *stuff*, we just zone out because we can't retain focus that long. However, when these same participants were told a story or shown a movie, their brains activated exactly as if the participants were *physically experiencing the story*.

Now if you think that sounds a little odd, just think about the last time you went to a scary movie or a movie that made you cry. I mean, be honest. When the alien jumped out at Sigourney Weaver, did you jump? I *still do* even though I know it's coming. I *still do* because my body doesn't know the difference. Even though intellectually, I know it's not real, that it's not happening to me, *my body doesn't know that.*

That again is the power of a story.

As human beings, we need story to figure things out; it's how we operate. When you share a story that says, "Here's what happened, here was the challenge, here's how I solved it, there's hope for the future," you've shared a message people will remember and use.

Story has always been how we entertain ourselves, and story is how we assert our humanity.

Want to use the power of story? Here are three things to keep in mind.

Align Your Stories With Your Values

Speak or write from your heart. If it doesn't move you, it won't move your audience.

Keep It Real

When I teach story, I emphasize a storyteller must *keep it real.* That doesn't mean the story can't be a metaphor or an analogy. It means you want to make it *as real* as possible for the person you're telling it to. (Remember, you want them to *feel* it with you, like those movies.)

You help them by sharing the experience through descriptions using at least three of the five senses: sight, sound, smell, taste, feel.

Keep It Simple

Keep control of your story and don't go on and on which doesn't necessarily mean a short story. Rather, you want to avoid telling more than one story at a time or trying to make multiple points in the same story.

When I teach a story workshop, there are always one or two folks who begin well and then go off on tangents. They start to tell their story and then they have to tell you *this one* because... WOW! this kind of impacted that...which reminds them of another story and...

They probably don't even notice but they've lost their audience or at the very least, getting impatient. I see the same thing happen in written stories and the reader skips over the redundant part, missing the heart of the message. Don't let this happen to you!

Your Invitation

If one of your goals is to use your business to transform the world around you, we're inviting you to submit your story to our next *Divas That Care* book. We want to help you inspire other women and find your tribe so we can all get up to great stuff!

If you're not sure where to begin, here are four places to help you find a good story. There are many more than these, but this is a good place to start.

1. First-hand Experience

First-hand experience is your most powerful source.

It's the story you find yourself telling over and over. The strength of a first-hand experience comes from how it touched your heart. You can honestly share how you felt, the change it made, what you're experiencing now, the struggle you went through to get there, the wisdom you gained and it's all *your story*.

People can argue against facts and figures all they want, *and they will*. We see it all the time. However, no one can argue with your personal experience without calling you a liar, and most people won't do that.

Your first-hand story is a real experience and a compelling source of hope. Telling your story from your point of view alerts your listener that if one person has done it, someone else can do it. You can honestly stand there and say, "If I can do it, anybody can!"

2. Witnessed Experience

The second story source is witnessed experience. This is the story someone shared with you or you observed. It's not quite as powerful as First-hand but close. If it's a very personal story, just be sure to get permission to share it. It's okay to change names to protect privacy as long as the facts of the story are true.

3. Metaphor or Analogy

For those of you who weren't paying rapt attention in your English classes, metaphor and analogy are when one thing represents something else.

Let me give you an example by sharing a story I tell people who ask me "What does a coach do?"

I use a metaphor story called "A Field of Diamonds" to answer the question and I freely admit borrowing it from Earl Nightingale.

"There was a poor farmer who was working his farm, but he dreamt of striking it rich by finding a diamond mine. So, he sold his farm, took the money, and set off to search for diamonds. Sadly, the man searched for years but never found what he was looking for.

Meanwhile back at the farm, the man who bought the place worked his fields faithfully. He was diligent and prospering, but not rich. One day, as he crossed a stream on his farm, something glittered in the water and caught his eye. Reaching down, he picked it up and pocketed it. Knowing his kids would enjoy it, he took it home and put it on the mantel of his fireplace.

It sat there for a long time until his geologist friend visited one evening. After dinner, his friend noticed the stone on the mantel and asked, "Where did you get that?"

The farmer replied, "My stream's full of them."

It turned out to be one of the biggest diamonds found up to that point in Africa, and he was *sitting on a field of diamonds*.

My job as a coach is to be that geologist and show you the possibilities you already possess and how to develop them."

Because you "get" how those farmers felt, you "get" what it is we can do together. You experienced the potential in a metaphor.

So, you've got a story and you want to step out as a Diva That Cares. Now what?

Simple. Submit your idea to us.

While the book you hold in your hands focused on how business created positive personal change, our next books in this series will focus outward to how we can transform the wider world around us. We need YOU to inspire other women with your experiences creating social impact using your business as a platform for change.

If you aren't already involved in social change but would like to be, figure out what gets your dander up because it's a good indicator of a problem you'd like to address. Then look at how you and your business can get involved. It could be directly, with a product or service or indirectly, by adopting a cause or volunteering. Now you've begun your story.

Once you have a story to share, here are some questions to help you tell it:

Why did THIS social problem catch your attention?

BUSINESS DIVAS THAT CARE

Why is it important to you?

Does your business address the problem directly (i.e. a green business to fight pollution)?

OR does your business give you the time freedom to work on creating change?

Send us an email at *DivasThatCare@gmail.com* with your ideas and let us help you get your message out there!

ABOUT APRILLE JANES

Aprille Janes spent 20 years as a successful business consultant to Fortune 500 companies like Coca Cola, Cardinal Health and Minute Maid. In 2003, she embraced her creative passion by helping people tell their story and connect on a heart level. She threw away her corporate suit, certified as a professional coach and became a published author and artist as well as a mentor to women entrepreneurs.

Today Aprille is a successful writer, artist, podcast host and small business strategist. Her mentorship helps women build successful businesses around their passion, live a life of purpose, and get noticed in a noisy and crowded marketplace. Her clients range from artists and writers to more traditional business models (and everything in between). Each is making a difference, doing what they love and making a great living.

Along with her husband and their crazy Jack Russell terrier, she enjoys the life of her dreams on the shores of the Bay of Fundy in Nova Scotia, Canada. Watching the tides ebb and flow from her living room windows reminds her to trust the rhythms of life.

CONNECT WITH THE AUTHORS

Candace Gish
www.divasthatcare.com
divasthatcare@gmail.com

Aprille Janes
www.AprilleJanes.com
Aprille.Janes@gmail.com

Pat Andersen
www.patandersen.com
patandersen@aol.com

Lorraine Crowston
www.LorraineCrowston.com
lcrowston@gmail.com

Brenda Hammon
www.brendahammon.com
spiritcreek@xplornet.com

Clara Ball
Clara.wemad@gmail.com

Erin Best
eerinbest@gmail.com

Tammy Boucher
followtammy@gmail.com

Camille Bowling
camillebowling@gmail.com

Cindy Chrenek
Cchrenek@gmail.com

Tammy Kirton
www.tammykirton.isagenix.com
tammykirton@gmail.com

Dana Pharant
www.InnerDominatrix.com
dana@danapharant.com

Charity Schaefer
www.charityschaefer.com
Charity.schaefer@yahoo.com

Teresa Syms
www.TeresaSyms.com
Teresa@sterlingsilvercoaching.com

Heather Andrews
followitthru@gmail.com

Amy McKenzie
Amymckenzie747@gmail.com

Benny Martin
beingbethanyjane@gmail.com

Candace Maruk
csmaruk@live.ca

Dianne Najm
diane@virtualgestures.com

Michelle Wright
farmcleanerupper@gmail.com

CPSIA information can be obtained
at www.ICGtesting.com
Printed in the USA
BVOW06s1045300817
493508BV00018BA/159/P